SPONSORSHIP IN MARKETING

Sponsorship of sports, arts, or events can be a powerful form of marketing communication for businesses and organizations. This book introduces the fundamentals of sponsorship-linked marketing, helping the reader to understand how sponsorship can be planned, executed, and measured. Drawing on original research, and exploring key theory, best practice, and cutting-edge issues, this is also the only book to fully explain how the *sponsor* can implement successful sponsorship campaigns and achieve their communication objectives.

The book covers every important conceptual and functional area of sponsorship in marketing communications, including:

- audiences, strategies and objectives;
- leveraging and activation;
- building sponsorship portfolios;
- measurement and evaluation;
- ambush marketing;
- managing relationships;
- internal audiences;
- public policy and legal issues.

Every chapter includes case studies, examples, and data from real organizations, businesses, campaigns, and events, vividly illustrating the link between fundamental principles and effective practice. No other book provides such a comprehensive, evidence-based introduction to sponsorship, demonstrating how organizations can connect *brands to real life*. This is essential reading for all students and practitioners working in sport marketing, sport business, events marketing, arts administration, business communication, or marketing management.

T. Bettina Cornwell is the Edwin E. and June Woldt Cone Professor of Marketing in the Lundquist College of Business at the University of Oregon. Prior to joining the University of Oregon, she was Professor of Marketing and Sport Management at the University of Michigan. Her research focuses on marketing communications and consumer behavior and often includes international and public policy emphases.

SPONSORSHIP IN MARKETING

Effective communication through sports, arts, and events

T. Bettina Cornwell

Routledge
Taylor & Francis Group

LONDON AND NEW YORK

First published 2014
by Routledge
2 Park Square, Milton Park, Abingdon, Oxon OX14 4RN

and by Routledge
711 Third Avenue, New York, NY 10017

Routledge is an imprint of the Taylor & Francis Group, an informa business

British Library Cataloguing-in-Publication Data
A catalogue record for this book is available from the British Library

Library of Congress Cataloging-in-Publication Data
Cornwell, T. Bettina.
   Sponsorship in marketing : effective communication through sports, arts
and events / by T. Bettina Cornwell.
      pages cm
   1. Corporate sponsorship. 2. Special events–Marketing. 3. Sports
sponsorship. 4. Performing arts sponsorship. I. Title.
   HD59.35.C67 2014
   659.2′85–dc23   2014001747

ISBN: 978-0-415-73979-5 (hbk)
ISBN: 978-0-415-73980-1 (pbk)
ISBN: 978-1-315-81637-1 (ebk)

Typeset in Bembo
by Keystroke, Station Road, Codsall, Wolverhampton

This book is dedicated to the home team,
Robert, Luke, David, and Steve, and our mascot, Comma.

CONTENTS

LIST OF FIGURES AND TABLES

Figures

Tables

PREFACE

This book on sponsorship focuses less on the "how to do it," and more on the "why it works." It summarizes recent research on sponsorship-linked marketing, providing direction and examples, along with the underlying theories and supporting research. My goal is to explain the inner workings of sponsorship to enable sponsors and sponsees to gain the most benefit from this form of marketing communication.

The book is organized for possible use in courses or seminars but is also intended for the business community. Those really new to the topics would want to read the basics (Part I), while those with more experience in the area could skip to the essentials (Part II) and move quickly to the advanced topics (Part III).

The book uses the "royal we" to denote many other researchers and commentators and myself. Although the book is written for the sponsor and from the view of the organization sponsoring sport, arts, or events, it is clearly useful for those seeking sponsorship and wanting to better understand the view of the other side.

In writing this book, I developed a greater appreciation for the preface as part apologia. In attempting to write an accessible book it was necessary to summarize and highlight research. In this process many interesting interactions and implications in the original research were not brought forward. My hope is that I did not in any way misrepresent the findings.

ACKNOWLEDGMENTS

As with many books, there may be one name on the cover but many people contributed to that possibility. First, I must thank Dr Helen Katz, Senior Vice President of Starcom MediaVest Group. Despite years of professional collaboration and even more years of friendship, I was still stunned when she offered to edit for me. Helen is a respected author. Her text *The Media Handbook: A Complete Guide to Advertising Media Selection, Planning, Research, and Buying* is in its fourth edition. She is an industry expert with a PhD in Communications and, I might add, has an undergraduate degree in English. Could one ask for a more talented editor? Still, her most important contribution to this book was her unflagging encouragement to the author to soldier forward.

My second editor for this book brought a different perspective. Karen Bonner, previous MBA student, research assistant, and now entrepreneur, having begun Red Duck Foods with classmates from the University of Oregon, provided a consumer perspective. Although working primarily on things like reference-style requirements and figures (when not seeking new venture funding and developing new packaging concepts), conversations and suggestions from Karen helped me improve the readability of the book. I also benefited from her positive outlook and her organizational skills.

A special thanks goes to Brian Eckert, Manager, Marketing Strategy and Operations, Global Marketing Communications, Aon Corporation, for providing information on their sponsorship program. Another thank you goes to Mark Phelps, JD, Senior Instructor Emeritus of Marketing, for his review of and comments on the "Ambushing and legal issues" chapter. Also, my appreciation goes to my long-time coauthor and friend Professor

Michael Humphreys, Department of Psychology, University of Queensland, for his comments on aspects of the chapter on "Memory for sponsorship relationships."

Additionally this book would not be possible without the work of colleagues and students. Much of their research is cited here. Naming individuals is nerve racking for the possibility of leaving someone out; nonetheless, I want to recognize, in particular, students with whom I have had the opportunity to work. In sponsorship research this includes: Monica Chien, Stephanie Cunningham, Ali Czafrann, Sarah Kelly, Krista Murray, Angela Maguire, Isabelle Maignan, Anna McAlister, David Nickell, Youngbum Kwon, Christopher Lee, Seung Pil Lee, Emerald Quinn, Donald Roy, Lars-Peter Schneider, Rachel Smith, Edward Steinard, Chanel Stoyle, Robert Van Ness, Clinton Weeks, and Taryn Wishart.

PART I

Background basics

1

HOW WE GOT HERE

In May of 2013, news broke that Levi Strauss, the popular denim jeans company founded in 1873, would put their name on the new San Francisco 49ers Stadium in California (Rosenberg 2013). The 20-year, $220 million agreement to call the 49ers football team's home the "Levi's Stadium" is not the most expensive naming rights deal but it is one of the most interesting. Why is it a good business idea for a maker of casual clothing to sponsor a football stadium for $11 million per year for 20 years? Only two decades ago, expenditure like this would have been unlikely, even unimaginable.

What does the iconic Levi's brand gain from their alignment with the 49ers Stadium? There is the typical signage on and around the stadium, luxury suites, access to the arena for their own events, and access to star players and even the coach. These "assets" of the deal are not, however, worth $11 million per year. What Levi's has purchased is a brand image boost, a reconnection to their San Francisco heritage in a modern form. The jeans market has become fragmented, with old competitors to Levi's such as Lee and Wrangler still in the picture, but with premium denim brands like True Religion and 7 For All Mankind making significant inroads.

Levi's relationship with the San Francisco 49ers allows them to tell new stories about the brand by leveraging the remainder of the advertising budget. With Levi's advertising budget of $80 million per year, the annual $11 million cost to connect with the also iconic 49ers seems more reasonable. Especially when one considers that this connection can differentiate the brand from its competitors and help it reach a youth market that is more keen on today's football than yesterday's gold mining history.

Sponsorship in marketing begins with an organization's investment in an event, person, or activity, typically with the expectation of recognition or collaboration that supports the marketing goals of the investor. Every year, sponsorship brings together a huge array of organizations and individuals that must align on points of interest for a contractual period. The sponsorship phenomenon is a cultural, social, and commercial plethora of connectivity. To understand sponsorship from a marketing perspective is to understand it as part of a full scale dynamic evolution taking place in communications.

The ascendency of indirect marketing

The ascendency of sponsoring as marketing communications activity is part of the rise of indirect forms of marketing (Cornwell 2008). Product placement in movie and programming, gamification, and the use of social media by brands are all movements in the same direction, namely away from mass communication "advertising" and toward integrated communication where the brand becomes part of the programming, part of the sharing, and part of the life experience.

The two words that describe and explain the rise of sponsoring and other forms of indirect marketing are "embedded" and "engaged." When a brand name is at the heart of the action, on a player's uniform, or in the hand of the actor on the screen, it comes alive and, importantly, it is difficult to edit out of the picture. Embeddedness is particularly valuable in sport given consumers' desire to see live programming in real time. It is the case that many a game has been recorded but unlike other entertainment programming, real-time engagement with sport tends to drive viewers toward immediate rather than delayed viewing. There is, however, growth in other programming that has real-time connectivity.

For example, Coca-Cola looks to focus its TV ad spending on so-called DVR-proof events such as the Super Bowl and "American Idol." Since ad-skipping is so problematic, many companies have moved away from traditional advertising in situation comedies and pre-programmed dramas. The explanation from Coca-Cola is as follows (Goetzl 2012):

> "The 30-second spots on television (are) no longer the way to do it," said CFO Gary Fayard at an industry event. "You still do 30-second spots, but if you're like me, most of the television you watch, you record and when you then watch it, you skip over all the ads . . . (but) you will watch certain shows live because you want to be able to talk about them tomorrow when you go to work."

This logic seems to be writ large in the change of programming in the first decade of the 21st century. According to the global information measurement company Nielsen, there has been a dramatic shift in the top ten primetime broadcast TV genres (Nielsen 2011). For the 2001–2 television season, general drama (29.5%) and sitcom (38.9%) programming dominated over reality (22.4%) and sport (9.2%). By the end of the decade, the 2010–11 season showed reality (56.4%) and sport (20.0%) dominating over general drama (32.7%) and sitcom (0%) in top ten programming.

The death of traditional advertising was predicted to be at the hand of technology (Rust & Oliver 1994). While advertising has not died, it has morphed and, in many instances, it has become the handmaiden of sponsorship. One could say sponsorship is, in many industries, the tail that wags the advertising dog. Sponsorship investments often dictate collateral advertising expenditures and creative platforms. Many discussions of the evolving communications landscape can be found and they share a set of converging factors of change (Cornwell 2008):

1. *Advertising avoidance*—technology that allows people to edit out advertising content is considered to be the main driver in the changes found in promotional budgets.
2. *Engagement*—technology allows people to have multiple forms of engagement simultaneously.
3. *Lifestyle*—people around the world with increasing discretionary income are spending more time in out-of-home activities such as attending performing arts and live spectator sports.
4. *Differentiation*—an abundance of product and price information pushes products and services toward perceived parity. Brands need points of differentiation and connection beyond product features and benefits.

Sponsorship growth

Sponsorship growth has been steady and has been only slightly influenced by downturns, at least in terms of overall spending (see Figure 1.1). There is considerable plasticity in sponsorship figures since each deal is negotiated even in times of economic pressure, so prices may decrease and influence apparent patterns, while the number of sponsorship contracts might actually rise. ZenithOptimedia (2013) estimated global advertising expenditures to be $505 billion in 2013. In the same year sponsorship spending worldwide exceeded $53 billion (IEG Sponsorship Briefing 2013). Thus, while sponsorship spending is dwarfed by advertising spending, it at the same time fuels and directs the nature of it.

Other indirect marketing activities have also grown. Brand placement in movies and television programming, in video games, and online games is poised to expand. From a base of $8.2 billion spent in 2012 on global product placements, forecasts are for near doubling by 2016 (*Research and Markets*

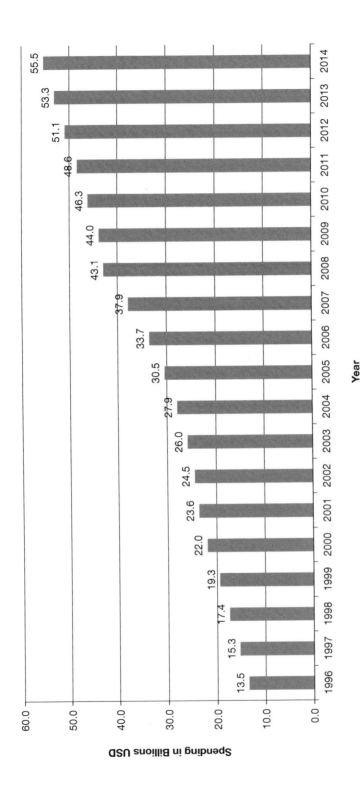

FIGURE 1.1 Growth in global sponsorship spending

Source: Based on IEG Sponsorship Briefing (2013).

2012). Mobile advertising embedded in games is growing quickly, with sales of mobile ads increasing from $0.6 billion in 2010 to $3.4 billion in 2012 (Mintel 2013). Social media ad spending is estimated to be nearly $11 billion by 2017, from the 2012 base of $4.7 billion (Stambor 2013).

These promotional activities and other "below the line" marketing programs are poorly documented. Even the name "below the line" suggests it is difficult to find the statistics needed to assess growth. Another name given to non-traditional communication paths is "unmeasured media." This historical nomenclature stems from the fact that measured media (TV, radio, and print) was measured by commercial suppliers whereas sales promotion communications were not.

Growth in properties

"Property" is a word typically used in sponsoring to denote the event, activity, organization, or person being sponsored. The shorthand use of "property" comes from the legal term "property rights holder." It signifies the legal entity that has the rights to protected symbols or trademarks as well as production or broadcasting rights. It is this legal entity or their representative that has the authority to enter into a sponsorship agreement. Before an agreement has been signed, properties are also sometimes also called sponsorship seekers, or after the contract is signed, "sponsees."

Properties, or more precisely, activities and events we now think of as properties, have grown over the past three decades in two ways: sponsorship of new events, and increased expenditures on existing events. First, things that had not been sponsored previously became sponsored. When sponsorship grew largely via expansion in the 1980s and 1990s, events or activities were being sponsored for the first time. As an example, between 1985 and 2000, 49 US sports stadiums acquired corporate names (Clark et al. 2002), many for the first time.

We can also see similar growth in sponsorship of US collegiate football bowl games during the 1980s and 1990s. Some notable title sponsor changes include the Peach Bowl becoming the Chick-fil-A Peach Bowl in 1998, and the Orange Bowl becoming the Federal Express Orange Bowl in 1989. While the Chick-fil-A Peach Bowl became simply the Chick-fil-A Bowl in 2006, the FedEx Orange Bowl changed hands and became the Discover (credit card) Bowl in 2010.

The second aspect of growth has been in sheer numbers. Based on listings of "major sports events" found on The-Sports.org (n.d.), Figure 1.2 was compiled. While the term "major sports events" was not defined, representative examples in 2013 include the European Allround Speed Skating Championships in the Netherlands, the Snooker Masters in the UK, the

Waterskiing World Games in Colombia, the Modern Pentathlon World Championships in Taiwan, the Judo World Championships in Brazil, the Archery World Championships in Turkey, and the World Powerman Duathlon Championships in Switzerland.

Global management consulting firm, A. T. Kearney, in its analysis of the global sports market, reports "A country-by-country breakdown finds that the sports industry is growing faster than GDP both in fast-growing economies, such as the booming BRIC nations (Brazil, Russia, India and China), and in more mature markets in Europe and North America" (Zygband & Collignon 2011). These analysts also note that there has been a shift in the way in which sport properties are monetized, from gate revenues such as ticket sales, to media and marketing rights. As well, there has been a growth in content packaging, the preparation for broadcasting and streaming, for both the sport property and the sponsor.

It is not only sports events that have increased in absolute numbers, as other live events have also grown. For example, music festivals have grown to be $1.4 billion and $4.6 billion industries in the UK and US, respectively. Interestingly, reasons for growth in live music events are due in part to digital media and the growth of replication and piracy, which have driven down revenues from recorded music (Grose 2011). Still, for many of the reasons already mentioned there is an expanding repertoire of opportunities for engagement through sponsoring.

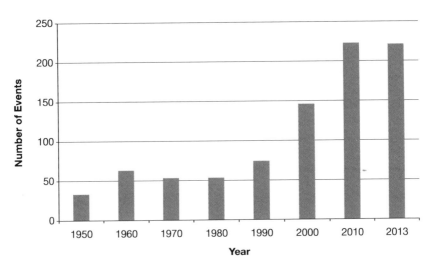

FIGURE 1.2 Number of major sports events worldwide

Source: The-Sports.org (n.d.).
Note: "major sports event" is not defined by this source.

Markets, brands, and sponsorship

In addition to consumer and technology trends that have supported the growth of sponsorship and changed the growth trajectories of properties, the communication goals of brands have also fueled sponsoring. World brands seek world communication platforms. There is no fully global media; even the Internet has limitations. Brands typically seek to parallel their communications with their distribution and thus seek national or global platforms. Thus, the Super Bowl is a valued sport event since it is the most watched sporting event in the US with 111.5 million viewers in 2014, but it still does not reach a world market. Super Bowl numbers pale in comparison to World Cup Soccer, which had 3.2 billion viewers in 2010, or half the world's population (FIFA.com 2011), thus making it at least a short window of something like global media.

It comes as no surprise that the location of the 2014 Winter Olympics in Sochi, Russia, and the location of the 2016 Summer Olympic Games in Rio De Janeiro, Brazil, are in two of the "Big Four" economies of economic growth. Likewise, the FIFA World Cup 2014 in Brazil, and 2018 in Russia follow a similar pattern. Sponsor interest in market entry and awareness are known to weigh into the host bidding process. Sponsorship of world–class events functions like a media vehicle, despite not yet being a specific medium.

With the goal of creating a new "media vehicle," IMG Worldwide, through strategic acquisitions in 2007 and 2010, made it possible to buy US college sports sponsorships at a national level. Before IMG College and competitors such as Learfield Communications were developed, if a brand wanted to sponsor a collegiate sport it would have to negotiate individual contracts with each college or university of interest. By negotiating representation of over 200 schools, IMG College allows brands to make one contract relationship and gain national coverage in their sponsorship portfolio. The significance of this has already changed the nature of collegiate sponsorship with many national brands investing in IMG's consolidated media rights offering.

The evolution of the industry

In addition to the sponsors and the properties, large media agencies are becoming highly visible due to their engagement in the sponsorship process. A look at some of these intermediaries gives a picture of the industry's evolution:

> *IMG Worldwide* is a global sports, fashion, and media business and talent representation firm. Originally focused on talent management and

known as the International Management Group, they have become a force in sponsorship. They represent over 1,000 individuals but at the same time offer a range of services so diverse as to allow one-stop shopping for many sponsors. While IMG has been acquiring companies in the business of sport and sponsorship regularly, one differentiating trend for IMG is the acquisition of properties such as the Great Open Road Marathon. Acquiring the properties themselves allows a measure of control not found in simply representing.

Octagon, part of the advertising conglomerate Interpublic Group, is a global sports, entertainment, and lifestyle agency. Their focus on sponsorship and entertainment marketing is oriented to professional sport teams, intercollegiate sports, broadcasting, and event management. Their sponsorship activations are heralded as being data-driven.

Creative Artists Agency was initially known for representing actors, but broadened their ambit to sports as celebrity endorsement and sponsorship fueled the interest in athletes. They now have CAA Sports that represents more than 800 athletes but also works with clients in areas such as licensing agreements, endorsements, and digital content, as well as broadcast rights, corporate marketing, and sponsorship sales.

IEG, previously International Events Group, now part of the multinational WPP advertising and public relations company, is known for keeping track of the worldwide sponsorship industry through their annual sponsorship report. IEG, while still focused on sponsorship information services such as webinars and online membership lists, has expanded their sponsorship analytics and evaluation services. They are differentiated by an orientation that includes products for both sponsors and sponsorship seekers, or properties.

Repucom, another large player in sport consultancy, provides market and media research and is known, according to their CEO, "as the best logo counters in the business" through their sponsorship exposure measurement services (Broughton 2013). Through aggressive acquisitions and international collaborations, the company, which began in 2004, now has more than 20 offices and 1,400 employees worldwide.

The phenomenon of corporate sponsorship has also spawned entrepreneurial cottage industries that could not have been imagined only a decade ago. For example, the National Sports Marketing Network has thousands of individual and corporate members. Some examples of the needs being met by the creative, void-filling entrepreneurs include: developing experiential programs and sponsorship activation (e.g., Velocity Sports & Entertainment, Fast Horse, Redpeg), providing sport-specific marketing measurement (e.g., Millsport in motorsports), managing and marketing audiovisual rights (e.g., Lagardère's Sportfive), sponsorship-linked advertising (e.g., M&C Saatchi Sport & Entertainment), sponsorship research (e.g., Sponsorship Intelligence) networking, and sponsor–sponsee matching services (e.g., Sponsorpitch), to name only a few.

Smaller concerns appear and disappear and are acquired by larger entities as soon as the need for their service or product is clearly demonstrated. These intermediaries with the backing of larger concerns include but are not limited to those specializing in event marketing (e.g., Omnicom Group's GMR), sponsorship and marketing (e.g., McCann Worldgroup's Momentum-NA, Inc.), and sports and entertainment rights (e.g., Comcast-Spectacor Company's Front Row Marketing Services).

Where are we now?

Many would say that we are in the middle of a communications metamorphosis.

We are on the verge of a different era of media consumption measurement. It has always been problematic to understand all the instances when a particular individual has an exposure to a communication. The golden, but largely unobtainable metric has for many years been single-source data—measurement of media exposure and buying behavior over time for an individual. This is in contrast to information about a group of individuals where all that can be said is what a person does "on average." For example, the company long known as Arbitron, now Nielsen Audio, is a consumer research company that collects single-source data. The company began with a focus on radio but is now working on measuring exposure across platforms including broadcast, Internet, and mobile devices (Arbitron 2012).

This era also brings us the possibility of "Big Data." Big data has come to stand for data sets so large, complex, and messy that they require new approaches to processing in order to find meaningful patterns of information. With information that can be measured and collected from our reading on a Kindle or Nook device, our music listening on an iPhone, navigating and searching, we create big data (Marr 2013). comScore is a company that measures this sort of digital information.

Now, if we take single-source information and big data together and add an understanding of sports, art, and entertainment exposure, we have something that both a property and a sponsor can utilize. This is exactly what a recent project has done. Project Blueprint is a cross-platform audience measurement partnership of ESPN, Arbitron, and comScore. ESPN's Glenn Enoch describes the project:

> We have set-top box TV data from comScore, with demographics and out-of-home viewing informed by Arbitron's Personal People Meter panel. comScore supplies data for digital platforms: PC, smartphone and tablet. Radio is important to ESPN, and we get listening data from Arbitron. Users and usage from these five platforms are combined through data integration.
>
> *Marketing News (2013, p. 116)*

The new integration of information is not, however, limited to traditional suppliers of commercial research and media firms. Technology-enabled companies have the potential to link together data as a new service product. For example, telecommunications company Verizon uses wireless-enabled devices that can link to specific locations such as a sports arena or a restaurant following the game. "'Verizon sought to attract sports teams and venues as early clients of the service,' said Colson Hillier, VP of Verizon Precision Market Insights, because it's difficult to measure accountability of sponsorship messages" (Kaye 2013). While Verizon has device-specific information, they report aggregated data that depicts how many were at the game and how many went for hamburgers following it. This is accomplished by combining the Verizon data with information from consumer insights company, Experian.

Deepening of the relationship

That sponsorship makes good sense because television advertising is largely edited out now undersells the value of sponsorship. While embeddedness moved marketers to sponsorship, the potential to tell interesting stories has kept brands in sponsorship and seen their budgets in this area expand. The key challenge of sponsorship is how best to measure it. Better measures of specific sponsorship outcomes are sorely needed. Sponsorship has a somewhat loose coupling with exposure, which is part of the charm, but it makes accounting for effects a challenge. The melding of social media and sponsorship is one of the most important trends in sponsoring. Sponsoring teams, athletes, performers, and the arts provides the story, or the content for social interaction, that is lacking in many corporate social media attempts. Social media interactions provide the tracking that sponsorship currently lacks. It is the match up for the future.

References

Arbitron, Inc. and the Coalition for Innovative Media Measurement (2012). Arbitron and CIMM Single-Source, Three Screen Audience Measurement Pilot Reveal. Retrieved October 5, 2013 from http://cimmusorg.startlogic.com/wp-content/uploads/2012/08/A_XPPR.12.pdf.

Broughton, D. (2013). Repucom Continues Aggressive Expansion Strategy. *Sports Business Journal.* Retrieved November 19, 2013 from http://www.sportsbusiness daily.com/Journal/Issues/2013/09/02/Global-Special-Issue/Repucom.aspx.

Clark, J. M., Cornwell, T. B. & Pruitt, S. W. (2002). Corporate Stadium Sponsorship, Signaling Theory, Agency Conflicts and Shareholder Wealth. *Journal of Advertising Research, 42*, 6, 16–32.

Cornwell, T. B. (2008). State of the Art and Science in Sponsorship-linked Marketing. *Journal of Advertising, 37*, 3, 41–55.

FIFA.com (2011). Almost Half the World's Population Tuned in at Home to Watch 2010 FIFA World Cup South Africa. *FIFA.com*, July 11. Retrieved September 20, 2013 from http://www.fifa.com/worldcup/archive/southafrica2010/organisation/media/newsid=1473143/index.html.

Goetzl, D. (2012). Coke to Focus on Events, Loses Faith in 30-Second Spot. *MediaDaily News*, March 23. Retrieved October 5, 2013 from http://www.mediapost.com/publications/article/170853/coke-to-focus-on-events-loses-faith-in-30-second.html?print=

Grose, T. K. (2011). Live, at a Field Near You: Why the Music Industry Is Singing a Happy Tune. *Time*, November 14. Retrieved November 29, 2013 from content.time.com/time/magazine/article/0,9171,2098639,00.html.

IEG Sponsorship Briefing (2013). 2013 Sponsorship Outlook: Spending Increase Is Double-edged Sword. Retrieved December 30, 2013 from http://www.sponsorship.com/IEGSR.

Kaye, K. (2013). Verizon Uses Phone Data to Connect Dots for NBA Teams, Sponsors. *Ad Age.* Retrieved September 20, 2013 from http://adage.com/article/dataworks/verizon-phone-data-connect-dots-nba-sponsors/245178/.

Marketing News (2013). Backpage Executive Insights. *Marketing News*, June, 116.

Marr, B. (2013). Is This the Ultimate Definition of "Big Data?" *Smart Data Collective*, June 6. Retrieved September 20, 2013 from http://smartdatacollective.com/node/128486.

Mintel (2013). Mobile Advertising. *Mintel*, May. Retrieved November 27, 2013 from http://www.mintel.com/.

Nielsen (2011). 10 Years of Primetime the Rise of Reality and Sports Programming. Retrieved September 20, 2013 from http://www.nielsen.com/us/en/newswire/2011/10-years-of-primetime-the-rise-of-reality-and-sports-programming.html.

Research and Markets (2012). Global Product Placement Spending Forecast 2012–2016. Retrieved November 29, 2013 from http://www.researchandmarkets.com/research/dq643c/global_product.

Rosenberg, M. (2013). Levi's Stadium: 49ers' New Santa Clara Home Gets a Name in $220 Million Deal. *San Jose Mercury News*, May 8. Retrieved October 3, 2013 from http://www.mercurynews.com/ci_23198944/levis-stadium-49ers-new-santa-clara-home-gets.

Rust, R. T. & Oliver, R. W. (1994). The Death of Advertising. *Journal of Advertising*, *23*, 4, 71–7.

Stambor, Z. (2013). Social Media Ad Spending Will Reach $11 Billion by 2017. Retrieved November 29, 2013 from www.internetretailer.com/2013/04/12/social-media-ad-spending-will-reach-11-billion-2017.

The-Sports.org (n.d.). Retrieved November 27, 2013 from http://www.the-sports.org/statistics.html.

ZenithOptimedia (2013). Executive Summary: Advertising Expenditure Forecasts June 2013. Retrieved November 29, 2013 from http://www.zenithoptimedia.com/wp-content/uploads/2013/06/Adspend-forecasts-June-2013-executive-summary.pdf.

Zygband, P. & Collignon, H. (2011). The Sports Market. Retrieved November 29, 2013 from http://www.atkearney.com/paper/-/asset_publisher/dVxv4Hz2h8bS/content/the-sports-market/10192#sthash.Q0n11gZS.dpuf.

2
VIEWS OF SPONSORSHIP

Why sponsorship?

The word sponsorship has the basic meaning of one entity supporting or accepting responsibility in some way for another. In marketing contexts, this support or responsibility is often financial in nature. Sponsorship has been defined as an exchange between a sponsor and a sponsee whereby the latter receives a fee (or value) and the former obtains the right to associate itself with the activity sponsored (Cornwell & Maignan 1998). Quester & Thompson offer a definition of sponsorship (2001, p. 34), which was adapted from Meenaghan (1991). These researchers describe sponsorship as "an investment, in cash or in kind, in an activity, person or event (sponsee), in return for access to the exploitable commercial potential associated with that activity, person or event by the investor (sponsor)." Other definitions also refer to the sponsor gaining "exploitable" assets or acquiring commercial potentials from a property.

All early definitions tended not to see the full potential of sponsorship as a partnership. This is understandable in part since in most sponsorship relationships there are power asymmetries that stem from the fact that sponsees are often dependent on sponsors for financial viability. Significant power asymmetries influence the behavior and attitude of relationship participants. Sponsors often dictate the terms of the relationship, even if it is not in their best interest to do so. Early on, sponsorship was much akin to buying promotions, sweepstakes, or trade show participation.

Many have argued that sponsorship is more akin to a "co-marketing alliance" (Farrelly & Quester 2005a), "cross-sector partnership" (Seitanidi &

Crane 2009), or "marketing partnership" (Meenaghan 2002). Importantly, on both sides, organizations and properties of all kinds refer to the other as "partners." Under this thinking the relationship is mutually beneficial, a two-way street, and not a relationship where one group exploits another.

In sport marketing, these "alignment-based marketing strategies" (Fullerton & Merz 2008) include four key categories: sponsoring, venue naming rights, endorsements, and licensing agreements that are commonplace in sport (see Table 2.1). While the fine arts have also seen extensive venue naming deals (for example, American Airlines Theater in New York, and Auditorio Coca-Cola in Monterrey, Mexico) the expression of sponsoring, endorsement, and licensing activities takes a different, somewhat less commercial tone in the arts. Even though these relationships have varying contractual details, they are often referred to as sponsoring (e.g., stadium rights sponsoring, athlete sponsoring).

TABLE 2.1 Alignment-based marketing strategies

Strategy	Example
Sponsoring	Red Bull energy drink sponsorship of the Major League Soccer Team, the New York Red Bulls
Venue Naming Rights	Etihad Airways Stadium in Eastlands, UK, the home of Manchester City
Endorsement	Old Spice men's personal care products and Baltimore Ravens linebacker Ray Lewis
Licensing Agreement	Mattel Hot Wheels toy cars and NASCAR

Source: Adapted from Fullerton & Merz (2008).

So why persist with the term sponsorship? There are at least two good reasons to refer to the nature of the engagement as sponsorship rather than partnership. First, there are so many types of partnerships in business and society that the term sponsorship can add clarity; it differentiates the discussion when one describes the relationship as a sponsorship. Second, it is actually descriptive of the relationship. Across many countries "partnerships" are legally recognized relationships were two entities come together and each contributes to the partnership and each is expected to share in both gains and losses stemming from the partnership. In contrast, the vast majority of sponsorship relationships are negotiated contracts or agreements of support from one entity to another. In this sense, the term sponsorship agreement serves well.

An account from a non-profit's struggle with the term partnership helps illuminate this. Concern Worldwide, an international humanitarian organization, wanted to address the definition of partnership for their organization. They brought 25 of their country representatives together to discuss the idea of partnering. Their poverty alleviation work around the world brought them into contact with various types of groups and community-based organizations. Exploration of partnerships at Concern Worldwide revealed two continuums that helped them map relationships: the level of collaboration and the level of shared values.

What they concluded was that a partnership did not need to rely on an agreement but was based on the relationship. Representatives at Concern Worldwide found that "staff tended to refer to organizations as 'partners' when the relationship exhibited characteristics such as honesty, mutual respect, interdependence, accountability, openness, trust, and transparency" (O'Sullivan 2010, p. 736). In summary, it makes sense that sponsorship is based on an agreement or contract, but the extent to which it becomes a true partnership is up to the individual actors and the resulting relationship quality.

Simple sponsoring versus sponsorship-linked marketing

Simple sponsoring, as one finds in the sponsorship of broadcast television, radio programming, and Internet content, is similar to advertising. Some researchers argue that the difference between content sponsoring and advertising is that "advertising changes the consumer's perception of a specific product while sponsorship changes the consumer's perception of a specific sponsor"—which can rub off positively on the brands of that sponsor (Harvey et al. 2006, p. 399). This point may have to do with the fact that content sponsoring is typically at the corporate rather than the brand level, but is nonetheless true.

The central focus of content sponsorship is typically some exposure in the sponsored programming or in the advertising in and around the programming. An excellent example is the long-term sponsorship of New York's Metropolitan Opera broadcasts by oil company Texaco. These simple sponsorships may be augmented with a viral campaign or with other collateral marketing, but they function like an integrated marketing communications plan with media coverage as the main mass communications goal. In fact, one study examining the lift in awareness from Internet content sponsorship found dramatic change in the willingness to consider a brand when it is presented as a sponsor of content without associated or other advertising on the same page (Harvey et al. 2006). Like the sponsorship of sports, arts, and events, content sponsoring can have a less commercial image relative to traditional advertising, but this is not guaranteed.

Sponsoring events and activities is typically different from sponsoring content. This difference is more apparent if the sponsor's goal extends beyond simply obtaining media coverage, which is typically the case. There is often an engagement at the event or involvement with activities that promote the brand. Helpful in this distinction is the term "sponsorship-linked marketing," defined as "the orchestration and implementation of marketing activities for the purpose of building and communicating an association (link) to a sponsorship" (Cornwell 1995, p. 15). Sponsorship of sports, arts, events, and activities can be just the starting point to building a marketing platform. Without leveraging this initial investment, the true potential of sponsorship can remain unrealized.

The sponsorship of individuals functions more like the sponsoring of events and activities than the sponsoring of programming. Many spokesperson contracts are, however, oriented around the individual's presence in advertising and this can limit the value of the sponsorship relationship. The sponsorship of individuals can be utilized for adding advertising theme and creativity. When the sponsorship of individuals is integrated with the sponsorship of activities and events, this gives the relationship a different tone. People connect with, follow, and emulate the behaviors of individuals. On the other hand, they may also despise and reject an individual for their professional or personal behavior.

Although it is difficult to gauge, the sponsorship of an individual permits a concentrated influence, be it positive or negative on the sponsoring brand. Take, for example, the 2009 scandal in golf when Tiger Woods' personal life was brought to public attention. It is estimated that the cost to Woods' sponsors in the 10–15 stock trading days following the scandal was a collective 2% of their value (Knittel & Stango 2014). Teams or events have multiple points of contact and while they may have negative elements, these may be offset or balanced by positive ones and thus, less extreme in their influence on sponsor perceptions.

The sponsored view

Here, the primary view taken is that of the organization sponsoring an event, activity, or "property." The term "property" is commonly used to describe "any organization (e.g., Manchester United), event (e.g., Super Bowl), or athlete (e.g., Tiger Woods) with whom a sponsor formally aligns itself as a vital component of its communications strategy" (Farrelly & Quester 2005a). Nonetheless, it is important to understand sponsoring from the perspective of the to-be-sponsored. Historically, the properties have viewed sponsorship as a funding mechanism. Some holders of property rights may also take a branding perspective on sponsoring partnerships but this has taken second place to the objective of securing sponsorships for financial support.

For the sport, art, charity, or event seeking sponsorship, the process typically revolves around the development of a sponsorship proposal that will be the backbone of a sponsorship presentation or pitch. Advantages to the property of having the proposal are that it helps to organize thinking and supports the stocktaking of property assets on offer. Disadvantages include that every would-be sponsor is offered the same or similar assets of the property as a smorgasbord from which the brand sponsor chooses. In this way, the standard proposal process can limit creativity regarding combining existing assets or developing new ones.

Sponsorship proposal elements typically include the following (Doherty & Murray 2007):

- rationale for the corporation to enter into a sponsorship agreement, which reflects its corporate objectives;
- description of the sport organization;
- demographics and psychographics of the participants and spectators;
- particular opportunities the sponsor can access (e.g., signage, product sales, hospitality opportunities, direct mail lists, television coverage);
- proposed length of the sponsorship agreement;
- amount of support desired;
- details on whether support is financial or in-kind;
- type of sponsorship that would be offered (e.g., exclusive);
- estimation of risks to the sponsor;
- current promotions/past results;
- planned evaluation.

One of the decision-making sticking points for properties is the price (amount of support) their assets can command. In a study of the asking price for 300 small and medium sport, charity, and arts/entertainment sponsorships the results showed that, as expected, media coverage drives the sponsorship asking price, as does attendance (Wishart et al. 2012) (see Figure 2.1). Interestingly, however, another variable that was influential in setting asking price was the extent of "access to property offerings" such as celebrities, venue and event images for advertising, and databases of customers. These proposal elements were found to be different from on-site variables such as logo placement, hospitality, and customer interaction potential. It makes sense that access to property offerings differently influence price because they can be used in marketing before the event.

True on-site elements that are confined to the event did not drive price but were rather expected or basic essentials of sponsoring. That is to say, one expects to get signage at an event, and while a sponsor would be surprised if it were not included, in this study it did not influence the asking price.

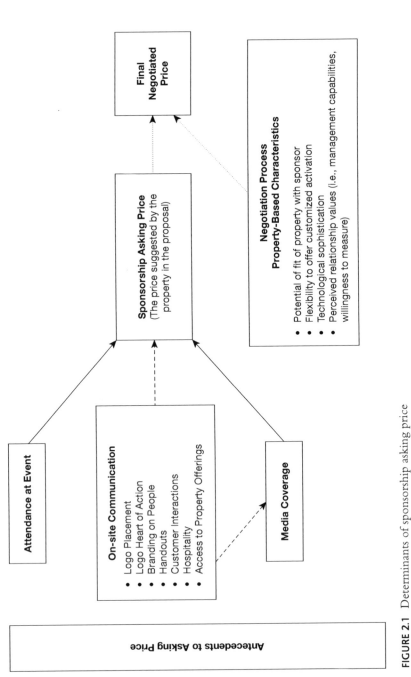

FIGURE 2.1 Determinants of sponsorship asking price

Source: Adapted from Wishart et al. (2012).

Note: Bold arrows show direct influence, dashed arrows show indirect influence, dotted arrows show influence on final negotiated price.

Importantly, the research only considered asking prices in publicly available proposals. The final negotiated price would give a clearer picture of what a sponsor values. In the negotiation process elements such as the degree of fit with the property and any customization or technological or relationship particulars that may make the property more valuable to a particular sponsor will influence the final agreed price.

In moving toward a partnership perspective, much of the advice about developing sponsorship proposals centers on understanding the potential sponsor. At the same time, properties often find it difficult to gain meaningful contact time with potential sponsors and to learn their communication needs. Managers of sports, arts, and events scan the environment for companies headquartered in the same city. They seek sponsors that have a functional or image match to the event or activity.

Doherty & Murray (2007) document the challenge of securing and maintaining sponsors for a small non-profit, Synchro Canada, a synchronized swimming organization. As is often the case with small properties, Synchro Canada did not feel they had much control in the sponsorship process since they had to be accommodating and appealing to potential sponsors. The researchers also document another typical challenge of small properties and that is having "too many small sponsorships" that require just as much service as those making a larger financial commitment (Doherty & Murray 2007, p. 53).

Importantly, large properties, such as arenas, often engage the services of a third party. These intermediaries represent athletes or properties when they seek sponsorship relationships. With the focus on developing financial support for the property, these intermediaries seek the best possible price for endorsement, naming rights, and sponsorship. If a mercenary view of sponsor support is taken, the most money may be gained but with a corresponding loss of fit, relationships, and long-term potential.

The sponsor's view

Awareness and attitude

From the sponsor perspective, especially among corporations, sponsorship is typically a communications platform or, if fully developed, a brand engagement platform. International Events Group in their 13th annual survey of sponsorship decision-makers (IEG 2013 Sponsorship Decision-Makers Survey 2013) found the most evaluated metrics in sponsorship to be:

1. awareness of company's/brand's sponsorship;
2. awareness of products/services/brand;

3. attitudes toward brand;
4. amount of media exposure generated;
5. response to sponsorship-related promotions/ads;
6. product/service sales;
7. customer/prospect entertainment;
8. employee/internal response;
9. lead generation;
10. response of trade channel partners;
11. lower customer acquisition costs.

As can be seen from this list, the vast majority of sponsors view their relationship with a property as a brand communication platform from which brand awareness and attitudes are developed. That said, there are myriad other concerns that go into the decision to sponsor.

Exclusivity

The possibility to be the only brand in a category communicating in conjunction with a property is one of the attractions to sponsoring. Early research from Canada, on understanding the sports sponsorship process from the corporate perspective, found exclusivity arrangements to be the most valued criteria when selecting sponsorship opportunities (Copeland et al. 1996). In the two decades since this research was conducted, the opportunities for and nature of exclusivity has changed considerably.

As sponsoring grew, properties realized that all-encompassing exclusivity categories such as "beverages" did not allow them to develop as many relationships as when considering alcoholic beverages, sports drinks, soda, and bottled water as individual categories. On the other hand, brands with offerings in all these subcategories would not want to buy individual sponsorships (at least not without a price concession). Exclusivity arrangements also have become more complex due to increasingly varied levels of property sponsorship. For example, in the United States, the National Football League (NFL) has league level sponsorship; sponsorship of iconic events like the Super Bowl competition, as well as team level and broadcast sponsors, not to mention the fact that games are played in a variety of sponsored venues. These layered sponsorships can generate additional revenues for the sport, as in the case of beer sponsorships of the NFL, but run the risk of consumer confusion and sponsor alienation (Fortunato & Melzer 2008). Thus, while sponsors value exclusivity, they also recognize the communication potential of properties and when choosing between exclusivity and the opportunity to link with a sought after property, even with competing sponsors at other levels, may choose the latter.

Relationships

In a series of studies, Australian researchers Francis Farrelly and Pascal Quester (2005a, 2005b) looked at relationships in sponsorship as co-marketing alliances. Their work with Australian Football League (AFL) sponsors found that, as with many business relationships, commitment and trust are central elements. What was particular for sponsoring relationships was that commitment, measured by additional spending on sponsorship investments, also termed "leverage," is a key determinant of economic satisfaction and trust. Commitment supports both economic satisfaction and social/psychological satisfaction in the sponsorship relationship. While commitment starts with the sponsorship "deal" or the initial contract, the additional spending to build the relationship is optional, and a sign of investment.

In a second study involving both sponsors and sponsees of AFL, their interviews revealed an understanding of the potential of co-marking relationships but they note that:

> ... major obstacles appear to exist that prevent sponsorship from realizing its full potential as a co-marketing alliance, including discrepancies in the strategic intent of the partners and insufficient time to establish goal convergence in the early stage of the relationship. Furthermore, contrasting levels of commitments may result in a perceived inequity in terms of economic satisfaction, eventually encouraging sponsors to go it alone in their sponsorship related decision-making.
>
> *Farrelly & Quester (2005a, p. 61)*

Nonetheless, it is the development of relationships that makes sponsoring different from standard marketing and part of the base of its vast potential.

Views of sponsorship: Particular determinants

Being a sponsor or being sponsored shapes the main dividing line in one's view of sponsorship. As noted, in general, properties seek financing and sponsors seek brand building, but more could be said about these entities and how they behave. One approach could be to look across industries that sponsor—banking, soft drink, telecom—and across properties to be sponsored—art, sport, charity. For instance, financial institutions tend to sponsor stadiums and arenas in part because the financing of the facility might be direct business and because sponsoring these sorts of structures can signal success (Clark et al. 2002). While it is interesting and informative to look at particular industries' activity trends, it is perhaps more useful to look at the characteristics that shape behavior and determine the entity's view of sponsorship.

Determined by scale

Small-scale or "grassroots" sponsorships across sport, the arts, charity, environment, and other areas typically have a local community focus. In fact, one study of small-enterprise sponsorship of regional sport tourism events found that one of the most prevalent objectives was "giving back to the local community" (Lamont & Dowell 2008). The natural reciprocity of small-scale sponsoring stems from the shared destiny and history of partners.

Another possible but by no means guaranteed characteristic of many small-scale sponsorships is authenticity. Large, often corporate sponsors seeking the authenticity of small-scale and local sponsorship relationships typically employ a community sponsorship strategy where an amount of support is delegated to local decision-making. From this money a business unit or a store manager can decide on the activities in his or her community that best match to the particular location. This may take the form of a foundation or an initiative referred to as identified philanthropy.

Advantages of community sponsorship portfolios include the aforementioned authenticity and sense of community building. The disadvantages could include a loss of brand meaning clarity as divergent relationships bring different meanings to the brand. In contrast, large-scale, world-class sponsorships are primarily about media coverage: high-profile examples include Formula One auto racing, Polo at Palermo Argentina, Wimbledon tennis, the Rugby World Cup, and the Tour de France. Depending on the sponsor they may also have a grassroots component but the media coverage sets the tone and forces some aspects of image unity.

Determined by focus

What do experimental theaters and lacrosse have in common? The answer is limited appeal and even more limited media attention. These focused properties tend to have a narrow range of sponsorship investors and are simultaneously more dependent on these relationships since they do not have revenues from large media broadcasting contracts (Greenhalgh & Greenwell 2013). However, niche sports and unique arts programs provide value to sponsors by offering access to a particular type of viewer or attendee. For example, Columbia sporting apparel and Merrell footwear sponsor "The Muddy Buddy" and the "Down & Dirty" mud runs, respectively, allowing the companies to reach enthusiasts for their products (Carone 2012). Likewise, Subaru, the four-wheel drive automaker, sees a match between mud runs and their sporty cars. To activate this linkage they provide a human car washing experience at the event where participants are cleaned up as they cross the finish line.

Determined by geographical region

Several researchers have begun to explore the role regional connectivity plays in the perceptions of sponsorship (Meng-Lewis et al. 2013; Woisetschläger et al. forthcoming). If the firm or its brands are strongly identified with a region then the logic is that they are part of an in-group and therefore more acceptable as a sponsor to sports, arts, or entertainment. The main concern is that out of market brands sponsoring cultural icons can be seen as commercial and opportunistic.

Scale, focus, and regional connectivity are only three characteristics that can shape the potential of sponsorship relationships. Clearly demographics, lifestyle image, projected social values are others that determine partnership boundaries.

The sponsor and the sponsee naturally take distinctive views on their shared relationship. Although not meaningfully documented in research studies, one can see that the extent to which each partner comes to know and understand the other, the more it serves the potential of the relationship. This presupposes a time commitment to sponsoring that is not seen in practice. For this reason alone, longer-term sponsorship relationships have an advantage since they allow time for partners to develop insight to the other side of the relationship.

References

Carone, C. (2012). Beyond the Olympics: Why Niche Sponsorships are Gold. *Forbes*, August 7. Retrieved November 23, 2013 from http://www.forbes.com/sites/christacarone/2012/08/07/beyond-the-olympics-why-niche-sponsorships-are-gold/.

Clark, J. M., Cornwell, T. B. & Pruitt, S. W. (2002). Heroes in the Boardroom? Corporate Stadium Sponsorship and Shareholder Wealth. *Journal of Advertising Research*, *41*, 6, 1–17.

Copeland, R., Frisby, W. & McCarville, R. (1996). Understanding the Sport Sponsorship Process from a Corporate Perspective. *Journal of Sport Management*, *10*, 32–48.

Cornwell, T. B. (1995). Sponsorship-linked Marketing Development. *Sport Marketing Quarterly*, *4*, 4, 13–24.

Cornwell, T. B. & Maignan, I. (1998). Research on Sponsorship: International Review and Appraisal. *Journal of Advertising*, *27*, 2, 1–21.

Doherty, A. & Murray, M. (2007). The Strategic Sponsorship Process in a Non-Profit Sport Organization. *Sport Marketing Quarterly*, *16*, 49–59.

Farrelly, F. & Quester, P. (2005a). Investigating Large-scale Sponsorship Relationships as Co-marketing Alliances. *Business Horizons*, *48*, 55–62.

Farrelly, F. & Quester, P. (2005b). Examining Important Relationship Quality Constructs of the Focal Sponsorship Exchange. *Industrial Marketing Management*, *34*, 211–19.

Fortunato, J. & Melzer, J. (2008). The Conflict of Selling Multiple Sponsorships: The NFL Beer Market. *Journal of Sponsorship*, *2*, 1, 49–56.

Fullerton, S. & Merz, R. (2008). The Four Domains of Sports Marketing: A Conceptual Framework. *Sport Marketing Quarterly*, *17*, 30–43.

Greenhalgh, G. & Greenwell, T. C. (2013). What's in It for Me? An Investigation of North American Professional Niche Sport Sponsorship Objectives. *Sport Marketing Quarterly*, *22*, 2, 101–112.

Harvey, B., Gray, S. & Despain, G. (2006). Measuring the Effectiveness of True Sponsorship. *Journal of Advertising Research*, December, 398–409.

IEG 2013 Sponsorship Decision-Makers Survey (2013). Survey: Sponsors Require More Agency Support, Spend Less on Activation. Retrieved December 30, 2013 from www.sponsorship.com.

Knittel, C. R. & Stango, V. (2014). Celebrity Endorsements, Firm Value, and Reputation Risk: Evidence from the Tiger Woods Scandal. *Management Science*, *61*, 1, 21–37.

Lamont, M. & Dowell, R. (2008). A Process Model of Small and Medium Enterprise Sponsorship of Regional Sport Tourism Events. *Journal of Vacation Marketing*, *14*, 3, 253–64.

Meenaghan, T. (1991). The Role of Sponsorship in the Marketing Communications Mix. *International Journal of Advertising*, *10*, 35–47.

Meenaghan, T. (2002). From Sponsorship to Marketing Partnership: The Guinness Sponsorship of the GAA All-Ireland Hurling Championship. *Irish Marketing Review*, *15*, 1, 3.

Meng-Lewis, Y., Thwaites, D. & Pillai, K. G. (2013). Consumers' Response to Sponsorship by Foreign Companies. *European Journal of Marketing*, *47*, 11/12, 1910–30.

O'Sullivan, M. (2010). Is This a Partnership or a Relationship? Concern Worldwide Maps the Difference. *Development in Practice*, *20*, 6, 734–39.

Quester, P. G. & Thompson, B. (2001). Advertising and Promotion Leverage on Arts Sponsorship Effectiveness (1998 Adelaide Festival of the Arts). *Journal of Advertising Research*, *4*, 33–47.

Seitanidi, M. M. & Crane, A. (2009). Implementing CSR through Partnerships: Understanding the Selection, Design and Institutionalization of Nonprofit-Business Partnerships. *Journal of Business Ethics*, *85*, 413–29.

Wishart, T., Lee, S. P. & Cornwell, T. B. (2012). Exploring the Relationship between Sponsorship Characteristics and Sponsorship Asking Price. *Journal of Sport Management*, *26*, 4, 335–49.

Woisetschläger, D. M., Haselhoff, V. & Backhaus, C. (forthcoming). Fans' Resistance to Naming Right Sponsorships–Why Stadium Names Remain the Same for Fans. *The European Journal of Marketing*. Retrieved April 3, 2014 from http://www.academia.edu/4549978/FANS_RESISTANCE_TO_NAMING_RIGHT_SPONSORSHIPS_-_WHY_STADIUM_NAMES_REMAIN_THE_SAME_FOR_FANS.

3

SPONSORSHIP AUDIENCES, STRATEGIES, AND OBJECTIVES

In the overall strategic planning process, sponsorship has had to swim upstream for decades. Sponsoring was for a long time a tactical decision at the bottom of the strategic planning process similar to product trials and coupons. For some organizations this is still the case. For others, given the extent of their investment, the duration of relationships, and the evolving importance of this activity, especially in some marketing communications programs, sponsoring must move up in the strategic planning process.

Consider the following, likely familiar, strategic planning elements:

Mission is the big picture, the fundamental reason for being. One's mission statement should explain this "reason for being" to both internal and external stakeholders. The mission typically reflects the vision and values of the organization.

Objectives and Goals are terms that are often used interchangeably. They both refer to what is to be accomplished; they are destinations, aims, or ends that support the mission. If a distinction is to be made, it is perhaps most useful to think of objectives as goals made specific and measurable.

Strategy is the means by which goals and objectives are accomplished, the route to the destination. Strategies describe how to achieve goals and objectives through executing a plan and employing particular tactics.

Execution is the doing. Execution is where various aspects of the strategic planning process come together to fulfill the strategy. It requires coordinating and delivering a strategic plan involving particular tactics while staying connected to the organizational mission. Execution, sometimes called implementation, should include accountability, which requires the monitoring and measurement of progress toward objectives and goals.

Tactics are particular actions undertaken in executing a strategic plan.

When companies engage in sponsorships that are as expensive as a new investment in a processing plant, one can be confident that this should not be simply tactical. The question is: when does a company begin to incorporate sponsoring into their strategic analysis and planning? What evidence is there for a link between sponsorship and mission?

Cunningham et al. (2009) conducted a content analysis of the mission statements and online sponsorship policies of 146 Fortune 500 companies. They coded what the companies would and would not sponsor (e.g., sports, arts, entertainment, charity) and they coded mission statement categories such as focus on competitors, innovation, being the best, a focus on customers, diversity, value, ethics, an employee focus, being helpful, responsibility, and improving quality of life. After undertaking several statistical procedures including cluster, factor, and regression analysis, they found corporate values and identity, as reflected in mission statements, are important to sponsorship policies that companies communicate:

> Specifically, companies emphasizing financial success in their mission statements prefer to sponsor individual athletes, education, the environment and health-related activities. Alternatively, companies stressing the importance of employees demonstrate a propensity to sponsor team sports, entertainment, religious, community, charity and business related activities.
>
> *Cunningham et al. (2009, p. 65)*

The link between successful individual athletes and firms seeking financial success makes sense because one can easily see the individual striving to be his or her best; whereas sponsoring team sport makes sense for companies wanting to motivate and inspire employees to work together toward a goal. The overriding implication of the research is that either explicitly, or through the influence of corporate culture, there is connectivity between corporate mission and the sponsorships undertaken.

Basic objectives

A great many lists of sponsorship objectives can be found. Typical among these are:

- corporate/brand image enhancement;
- direct on–site sales;
- increased awareness levels;
- reaching specific target market;
- develop/build client relationship;
- gain media exposure;
- increase employee morale;
- trade/hospitality objectives;
- product/service demonstration platform.

One challenge in learning if objectives for the sponsorship have been met is that the direct relationship between exposure to sponsorship information and brand-related behaviors such as purchase or recommendation is hard to trace. In much the same way as it is difficult to connect an advertisement to any particular purchase, it is difficult to track the influence of sponsorship.

Sophisticated objectives

In addition to basic communication objectives, brand managers may set more extensive and comprehensive objectives for sponsorship. Top in this category would be utilizing sponsorship to differentiate the brand from competitors and to build brand equity. In business-to-business categories, objectives might include building employee identification with the firm through sponsorship or elevating brand perceptions with key clients. The more sophisticated objectives tend also to be longer term in nature.

An early question asked about sponsorship programs concerned their ability to build brand equity (Cornwell et al. 2001). Brand equity can be approached in many ways. According to David Aaker in his book *Managing Brand Equity* (1991), brand equity is a set of assets (and liabilities) linked to a brand's name and symbol that adds to (or subtracts from) the value provided by a product or service to a firm and/or that firm's customers. The four dimensions of brand equity are: brand name awareness, brand loyalty, perceived quality, and brand associations. Cornwell et al. (2001) surveyed managers who utilized sponsoring in their marketing platform regarding the brand equity-building potential of their sponsorships. While these were early days in sponsoring, two findings are worth noting. Sponsorship was found to be valuable in differentiating a brand from competitors and in adding financial value to the brand. Thus, sponsorship was viewed as a builder of brand equity. These results were qualified, however. The extent of active management involvement in sponsorship development was positively related to differentiating the brand from competitors and adding financial value to the brand.

Strategies

It has been proposed (Ryan & Fahy 2012) that sponsorship has evolved since the 1980s and that the priorities over time have shifted, in what can be seen as five distinct stages. Sponsorship is thought to have had a dominant approach initiated in the following order:

1. *The philanthropic approach*—pre-1980s, viewed sponsorship as a gift and with a strategic focus on broad corporate objectives and developing goodwill. Sponsorship management was seen as driven by the interests of CEOs without formal selection criteria for sponsorship or programmatic evaluation.
2. *The market-centered approach*—1980–90s, viewed sponsorship as an invest-ment. The hallmark of this era was a focus on brand awareness and the idea of sponsorship delivering a return on investment. Sponsorship management was characterized as marketing objectives-oriented, even media-oriented.
3. *The consumer-centered approach*—early 1990s on, viewed sponsorship as meaning creation. Here, there was an emphasis on learning how spon-sorship works in the mind of consumers (Cornwell et al. 2005). A shift was seen from management of media exposure toward gaining a deeper understanding of consumers and this orientation remains strong.
4. *The strategic resource approach*—late 1990s on, viewed sponsorship as a source of competitive advantage. Here sponsorship investments were recognized as insufficient for sustainable success and the need for further investment at the inter-organizational level was recognized. Ryan and Fahy (2012) note that "The strategic resource approach serves to move the emphasis from a conception of sponsorship as a purchase of an exploitable property to one in which the value of sponsorship is seen as generated and developed at the organizational and inter-organizational levels" (p. 1144).
5. *The relationship and networks approach*—early 2000s to present, views sponsorship as interaction. Two perspectives are encompassed here. The first perspective sees relationships as dyads between sponsor and sponsee as the focus. The network approach recognizes dyads but sees them as embedded within a larger web of relationships.

These authors see overlap amongst the approaches that have developed over time. From their review they suggest there has been a decline of the market-centered approach; a return to the philanthropic approach via corporate social responsibility; and continued importance of the consumer-centered, strategic resource, and relationship approaches. They also argue that the area of network approaches in sponsorship is underdeveloped.

The rapid development of the systems and intermediaries supporting sponsorship (Cornwell 2008) has led to a more complex context that is challenging for managers to negotiate. Ryan and Fahy (2012), following the logic of Möller and Halinen (1999), suggest four levels of sponsorship network management: exchange relationship level or dyads, relational portfolios such as those held by sponsors (Chien et al. 2011) and property rosters (Ruth & Simonin 2006), organizations in networks and the overall industry network. The challenge is that developing a networking ability that allows managers to connect their resources to those of others in a system is difficult (Ritter et al. 2004). It requires a level of mutual understanding that takes time, energy, and continuous reinvestment. Can an interim concept that does not demand a dynamic systems background be helpful?

Partnermix

Partnermix is not the latest dating or dance craze, but a term that could capture the apparent evolution of the promotions mix, the marketing mix, and new thinking on what might have been the business mix, had the term ever had currency. An interim definition of partnermix development is the selecting and combining of relationships across the network of entities in an organization's environment to forward strategic goals. This term, being proposed here, reflects the fact that many of our models of marketing communication do not reflect marketing actions, contextual realities, or complex inter-organizational relationships. A litany of examples could start with choice of retail location (a poor anchor store can spoil the mix), consumers that co-create products, relationship marketing, joint promotions, retail distribution with turnkey partners, and of course sponsorship. This implies a shift in business process—starting with the fact that the choice of business partners comes early in the decision process. A fundamental aspect of this partner-based thinking is the sense of shared fate.

As an example of partnermix networking potential, take the case of a new sponsorship where the first sponsor to sign an agreement, such as Levi's and the 49ers Stadium, has the opportunity to be in the property's conversation as additional sponsors are sought. There are advantages of seeking additional sponsors that while exclusive in a category, also connect in meaningful ways to both sport and fashion. One is made stronger or more vulnerable by choice of partners.

The idea of a strategic partnermix is naturally suited to sponsoring. Think of a single new sponsorship deal. It connects the company (likely with an existing portfolio of sponsorships) with a property that has an existing roster of sponsors. The new property might also come with existing beneficiary sponsorship relationships in addition to their roster of sponsors (e.g., the relationship between NBA and NBA Cares and a host of initiatives). The individual athletes in turn may have sponsorship contracts. Within this network, relationships to emphasize and nurture should be evaluated, since all available partners offer different strategic synergies. It is impossible to afford attention to all potential partners in this network, so a selective partnermix strategy based on current objectives and future goals could provide focus.

Tactics or execution

Online and in many "how to" books, one finds a superabundance of advice on tactics in sponsoring. Whether it is painting a mural on the rooftop of the New York Wine & Food Fest sponsored by the Blue Moon Burger Bash (Chaudhury 2013) or NASCAR auto racing driver, Shawn Johnson dancing with fans (developed by Fast Horse; Sponsorship Activation n.d.), there is no shortage in creativity and fun when it comes to activating sponsorships. Activations are the engaging tactics brands utilize to build audience involvement. The challenge is to make the activations brand (and property) relevant, unique so to be memorable and not confused with the activations of competing brands, and engaging so that they become part of the experience and not an addendum.

Lastly, at the tactical level, what happens at the event may be for some sponsorships the beginning and the end of reaching important audiences, but for many brands, the attending or participating audience is only a springboard for media audiences and online or mobile activations. If an event-based activation is exciting and newsworthy, it garners media attention. If the brand plans for it, on-site activation can also become the platform for concurrent or future social media leveraging.

Audiences

In sponsoring, we can identify five broad audience categories with associated interim communication processes and desired outcomes (Cornwell, 1995; Gardner & Shuman 1988). These five include consumers/customers, channel members, institutions (e.g., financial, non-profit), government and community leaders, employees and future employees (see Figure 3.1). Although a sponsorship relationship could be directed at any stakeholder group or

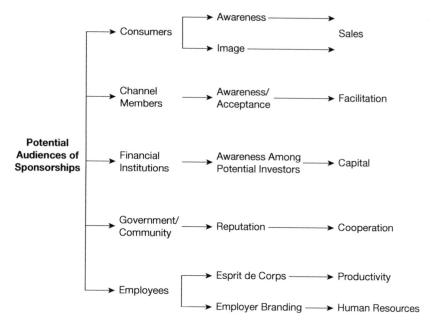

FIGURE 3.1 Sponsorship audiences and effects

Source: Adapted from Cornwell (1995). Based originally on Gardner & Shuman (1988).

public of an organization, overwhelmingly the interest has been focused on consumers.

Consumer audiences

Sponsorships are often utilized to reach a specific demographic. Courvoisier Cognac, for example, in seeking a younger, 25–35-year-old market has sponsored a series of music events and festivals including in the UK, the Brighton Festival, Secret Garden Party, and the Edinburgh Festival Fringe (Joseph 2012). Matching the demographics of brand consumers and a to-be-sponsored property's attendees is widely discussed as a typical approach in sponsoring, but is it always the right one?

Writing from the perspective of advertising management, Percy & Elliott (2005) make an important distinction between target audiences and target markets. They explain that markets are defined by the use of segmentation whereas target audiences are defined by their communications potential. Target audiences should be those individuals with whom we want to communicate due to their likely brand-related behavior. For instance, target-ing one's own brand loyal customer, or even the brand loyal customer of another brand, is less valuable than targeting an individual open to switching or beginning use of a product category.

Marketing communications, in order to be effective, should orient to target audiences and these might be a particular subset of consumers within the brand's overall target market. A solid example here would be in telecommunications—messages about selecting a brand should not be targeted to those already having a two-year contract with your brand or your competitor unless the message is associated with a way in which the consumer can break a contract.

The discussion of target audiences when taken into sponsorship becomes more complex and interesting. First, there is the target audience for the brand and then there is the audience for the sponsored property. The demographics question is, to what extent does the target audience for the brand overlap with the attending or viewing audience for the property? Moreover, if a brand manager is intent on finding a communications audience based on brand-related behavior, not simply demographics, how is it possible to pick out those potentially interested in the brand? This is where activation can play a critical role. At the 2011 Heineken Open'er Music Festival, the beer brand message was "Open Your World." During the festival in Poland, participants could sign up for a free QR code to be worn while at the event. Beer is a product consumed in social settings and the Heineken activation allowed people to put a message of their own out and allow others to connect (Sorrells 2012). Although the starting point for a meaningful partnership will naturally include basic demographics and psychographics, finding the best way to reach the brand's target audiences via sponsorship is by understanding brand-related behaviors.

Fans as audiences versus brand target audiences

In considering audiences for brands in sponsoring, it is essential to remember that the property brand has an audience as well. This is obvious in sports but again, there is an additional level of complexity of which to be aware. Bergkvist (2012) surveyed fans of the Stockholm AIK football team to learn about their perceptions of their sponsor's beer brand, Åbro, and their rival, Hammarby's sponsoring beer brand, Falcon. The two teams are big rivals and findings showed that there is a negative transfer of image from the rival Hammarby team to the brand sponsoring them, Falcon. This research suggests that any sponsorship of a competitive participant "in-group" that builds positive brand values may also come with a competitive "out-group" that may build negative associations to the brand. Admittedly, this is less likely in the absence of a strong basis for rivalry and also less likely for products not consumed in public but still worthy of managerial concern.

The oddly named tendencies of fans toward BIRGing or "basking in reflected glory"—experiencing vicarious achievement—and CORFing "cutting off reflected failure"—distancing from loss (Wann & Branscombe 1990) can help in understanding of the dynamics of sponsorships that involve intense fan behaviors. Basking in the reflected glory of team performance can spill over to the sponsoring brand; likewise distancing oneself from poor team performance might also influence sponsors. Fan passions can be directed toward anything related to the home team or the rival.

Schadenfreude is a feeling of enjoyment from seeing another fail. Thus, not only are fans of a team happy when their team wins, they are happy when their arch-rival loses. Researchers have shown that "schadenfreude is manifested toward a variety of targets associated with a rival team, including the team's sponsors" (Dalakas & Melancon 2012, p. 51). In short, team sports come with more than simply the fans of the sponsored team as a straight-forward audience for the sponsoring brand.

Channel members as target audience

Very little is written about how sponsorship targets channel members but the evidence abounds in practice. One way in which sponsorship visibly targets channel members is in the franchise model. For example, Chick-fil-A Restaurants, headquartered in Atlanta, Georgia, sponsors the Chick-fil-A College Bowl that is played annually in the same city. This American football event is held in the catchment of the restaurant chain's franchises and speaks not only to consumers but also to current and potential franchisors.

Another area where channel members are audiences for sponsorship is in events that are trade-focused. For example, Glutino, a gluten-free food company, sponsors the tradeshow, Natural Products Expo West. The event, now in its 33rd year, attracts over 60,000 people and 2,400 companies (Hillson 2013). This allows Glutino the chance to reach both distributors and suppliers at one event.

Community as target audience

Under banners such as "Community Giving," "Community Relations," and "Corporate Giving," one finds strategic philanthropy via sponsorship. Community sponsorship support is grouped by firms along with activities such as non-profit grant funding, gifts, scholarship, and volunteering activities of a company. With reflection one can see that the world recession sparked in the United States in 2007, and made global in 2009, changed the face of sponsorship, perhaps permanently. In tough economic times, corporate expenditures on seemingly extravagant sports and entertainment sponsor-ships were curtailed to favor more interest in community and charitable sponsorships or were combined with beneficiary sponsorships. IEG's survey of sponsors found companies planning more spending in arts and entertainment (31% and 31%) in 2012 than in 2008 (12% and 16% respectively) (IEG Sponsorship Report 2012).

This orientation to community sponsorships is associated with a trend in the development and expansion of corporate foundation giving. In 2011, corporate foundation giving grew faster than all other types (Lawrence 2012). In a trend analysis of million-dollar gifts complied by the Lilly Family School of Philanthropy (2013) at the University of Indiana, one can see that corporate foundations give to education, arts, culture and humanities organizations, environmental, health, and humanitarian service organizations. Corporate foundations tend to give much less to religious organizations than do individuals and non-corporate foundations. While giving was not all in the form of sponsoring, these areas of community support are typical in sponsoring.

Trends toward community and non-profit sponsoring also can be seen in many organizations as an area of decentralization. Local branches and business units are often allocated budgets that are earmarked for spending on local sponsorships. This supports community understanding and relationships but could also result in a diffuse brand image if the brand becomes involved in radically different sponsorships over time.

Financial institutions, governments, and NGOs as target audience

It should also be noted from the Lilly Family report on giving that corporate foundations also make gifts to international organizations, primarily in the areas of human services, public/societal benefit, health, education, and environment. Financial, non-governmental institutions play myriad roles in business decision-making. While not the exclusive domain of cause-related sponsorships, it is the case that cause-linked sponsorships in areas of social concern often must interact with governments and NGOs. There is much less written on addressing institutional targets with sponsorship.

Returning to the partnermix thinking, reaching multiple audiences and at the same time supporting multiple objectives is naturally the case in cause sponsoring. When a corporate sponsor, a non-profit NGO and government groups are working together, each has a different aim. The corporation may want to develop goodwill in a particular country while the government may want children to participate in sport and the non-profit may be the mechanism between the two. One of the challenges for the corporate sponsor, the non-profit, and government in this context is to evaluate the outcomes. The question is how to measure the social good of a sponsored program?

One area of research that has attempted to address this challenge is in the development of a scale that measures sport's contribution to society (Lee et al. 2013). The instrument was developed to help groups like the United Nations Sport for Development and Peace division. Both corporate enterprises and established sport properties welcome the opportunity to do good things and build their corporate social responsibility record. For-profit enterprises must, however, also be responsive to shareholders that seek to know how money not brought back as dividends is spent. Other groups also seek to measure the effectiveness of their programs. If the social value of sports, in particular in developing countries, can be demonstrated through measurement, then the thinking is that investment could be increased. In this way, measurement of social contributions in any area has the potential to allow communication with multiple audiences and benefit all partners.

References

Aaker, D. A. (1991). *Managing Brand Equity*. New York: The Free Press.

Bergkvist, L. (2012). The Flipside of the Sponsorship Coin: Do You Still Buy Beer When the Brewer Underwrites a Rival Team? *Journal of Advertising Research*, March, 65–73.

Chaudhury, N. (2013). New York Wine & Food Fest: 30 Clever Brand Activations from Delta, Pepsi, Groupon, and More. *BizBash*. Retrieved on November 27, 2013 from www.bizbash.com/new-york-wine-and-food-fest-30-clever-brand-activations-from-delta-pepsi-groupon-and-more/new-york/story/27345/#sthash.3aHeRmj2.dpbs.

Chien, M., Cornwell, T. B. & Pappu, R. (2011). Sponsorship Portfolio as Brand Image Creation Strategy. *Journal of Business Research*, *64*, 142–9.

Cornwell, T. B. (1995). Sponsorship-linked Marketing Development. *Sport Marketing Quarterly*, *4*, 4, 13–24.

Cornwell, T. B. (2008). State of the Art and Science in Sponsorship-linked Marketing. *Journal of Advertising*, *37*. 3, 41–55.

Cornwell, T. B., Roy, D. P. & Steinard, E. A. (2001). Exploring Manager's Perceptions of the Impact of Sponsorship on Brand Equity. *Journal of Advertising*, *30*, 2, 41–51.

Cornwell, T. B., Weeks, C. & Roy, D. (2005). Sponsorship-linked Marketing: Opening the Black Box. *Journal of Advertising*, *34*, 2, 23–45.

Cunningham, S., Cornwell, T. B. & Coote, L. (2009). Expressing Identity and Shaping Image: The Relationship between Corporate Mission and Corporate Sponsorship. *Journal of Sport Management*, *23*, 1, 65–86.

Dalakas, V. & J. P. Melancon (2012). Fan Identification, Schadenfreude toward Hated Rivals, and the Mediating Effects of Importance of Winning Index (IWIN). *Journal of Services Marketing*, *26*, 1, 51–9.

Gardner, M. P. & Shuman, P. (1988). Sponsorship and Small Business. *Journal of Small Business Management*, *26*, 4, 44–52.

Hillson, B. (2013). Natural Products Expo West Rocks. Retrieved October 13, 2013 from http://www.glutino.com/blog/natural-products-expo-west-rocks.

IEG Sponsorship Report (2012). Old Habits Do Die: Sponsor Survey Sees Less Reliance on Ads, Signage. Retrieved on November 29, 2013 from http://www.

sponsorship.com/iegsr/2012/03/16/Old-Habits-Do-Die–Sponsor-Survey-Sees-Less-Relian.aspx.

Joseph, S. (2012). Courvoisier Bids to Reclaim Luxury Status. *Marketing Week*, December 12, 10.

Lawrence, S. (2012). Foundation Growth and Giving Estimates: Overview of Foundation Giving through 2011. *Foundation Center*. Retrieved September 20, 2013 from http://foundationcenter.org/gainknowledge/research/pdf/fgge12.pdf.

Lee, S. P., Cornwell, T. B. & Babiak, K. (2013). Developing an Instrument to Measure the Social Impact of Sport: Social Capital, Collective Identities, Health Literacy, Well-being and Human Capital. *Journal of Sport Management*, *27*, 24–42.

Lilly Family School of Philanthropy (2013). A Decade of Million-Dollar Gifts: A Closer Look at Major Gifts by Type of Recipient Organization, 2000–2011. *Indiana University Lilly Family School of Philanthropy*, April, 1–29. Retrieved October 20, 2013 from http://www.philanthropy.iupui.edu/files/research/report_w_appendix_april_2013.pdf.

Möller, K. K. & Halinen, A. (1999). Business Relationships and Networks. *Industrial Marketing Management*, *28*, 413–27.

Percy, L. & Elliott, R. (2005). Selecting the Target Audience. In *Strategic Advertising Management*, pp. 63–85. New York: Oxford University Press.

Ritter, T., Wilkinson, I. F. & Johnson, W. J. (2004). Managing in Complex Business Networks. *Industrial Marketing Management*, *33*, 175–83.

Ruth, J. A. & Simonin, B. L. (2006). The Power of Numbers: Investigating the Impact of Event Roster Size in Consumer Response to Sponsorship. *Journal of Advertising*, *35*, 4, 7–20.

Ryan, A. & Fahy, J. (2012). Evolving Priorities in Sponsorship: From Media Management to Network Management. *Journal of Marketing Management*, *29*, 9/10, 1132–58.

Sorrells, M. (2012). Heineken Uses QR Code Stickers to Help Festival Attendees Connect with Each Other. *BizBash*, February 16. Retrieved November 27, 2013 from www.bizbash.com/heineken_uses_qr_code_stickers_to_help_festival_attendees_connect_with_each_other/new-york/story/22492/#sthash.Atg VRieZ.dpbs.

Sponsorship Activation (n.d.). *Fast Horse*. Retrieved November 27, 2013 from https://www.fasthorseinc.com/home/fast-horse-portfolio/sponsorship-activation/.

Wann, D. L. & Branscombe, N. R. (1990). Die-hard and Fair-weather Fans: Effects of Identification on BIRGing and CORFing Tendencies. *Journal of Sport and Social Issues*, *14*, 103–17.

PART II

Sponsorship essentials

4

HOW SPONSORSHIP WORKS

Cheering for the home team is found across sports and around the world. The Korean version of cheering is, however, rather special. For example, "newspaper cheering" involves cutting up newspapers and shaking them, whereas another popular form of cheering, "plastic bag cheering" involves tying an air-filled plastic bag that is of the team's colors to one's head (Kholic 2013). Importantly, large-scale cheering Korean-style is often organized and sponsored. Memorable in this regard is the Hyundai-sponsored street cheering of the 2010 World Cup games, which gained the company extensive media exposure. Is, however, a simple gain in media exposure the end point of our understanding about how sponsorship works?

Sponsorship is more than just media exposure and therein lays both the value and the need for deeper understanding of how it functions. Subsequent to the World Cup news of street-cheering media exposure gained by Hyundai, researchers have investigated if cheering can support perceptions that the sponsoring firm fits well with the event. Their findings showed that, in the Korean context, incongruent sponsors could improve their image of fit by sponsoring street cheering that fits with the event (Han et al. 2013).

In order to get the most from a sponsorship investment, it is valuable to understand how sponsorship works. To accomplish this, we can think about sponsorship as a communications platform, as a meeting place when using hospitality, as thematic inspiration for advertising, and as a starting point for online engagement in social media. Depending on the goals for the sponsorship, one needs to choose the best mechanism of delivery. To learn the inner workings or the "mechanisms" that deliver a particular outcome is to understand how to improve functioning. As in the street-cheering example, it is relatively easy to learn that street cheering provides media coverage but with closer inspection via research we also learn that it can function to increase fit between a sponsor and a property. If there is a goal to increase perceptions of fit, which are often associated with positive attitudes to sponsorship, we now know that in the Korean context, street cheering is one mechanism that delivers against this goal.

A communications-based model

With the goal of understanding the inner workings of sponsorship communication, we begin with a consumer-focused communications orientation, in which its elements and messages (explicit or implicit) are processed (see Figure 4.1). Although consumer-focused, this orientation also informs both hospitality and mediated sponsorship-linked marketing. Thus, we begin by breaking sponsorship down and considering it as a model of consumer-focused marketing communications.

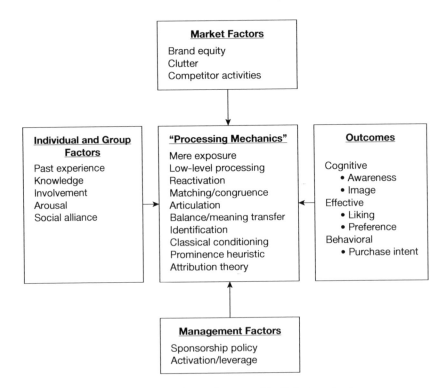

FIGURE 4.1 Model of consumer-focused sponsorship-linked marketing communication

Source: From Cornwell et al. (2005).

This model, originally published in the *Journal of Advertising*, brings together a decade of work on sponsorship (Cornwell et al. 2005). The model depicts a simplified five-element frame for understanding processing: individual and group factors, market factors, and management factors all influence the processing "mechanics" of sponsorship and subsequently the measured outcomes of the sponsorship. Each of these model boxes will be briefly reviewed.

Individual and group factors

Before any sponsorship communication is processed, it is known that people exposed to a sponsorship bring particular characteristics that may predispose them (negatively or positively) to your message. For example, individuals with considerable experience with and knowledge about your brand may need little or no information from a sponsorship except for the logo. Sponsorship exposures may serve as a reminder to buy for those already familiar. A high protein and carbohydrate bar like Powerbar, within the context of a marathon, would be known as a product typically consumed for energy; however, in other markets its use in sponsorship would need support from other communications to establish a base of understanding about its use. This is one of the reasons that sponsorships are rarely used as a stand-alone strategy in international market entry (Amis & Cornwell 2005), since without collateral advertising those not familiar with a brand and its category may essentially miss the message.

Individual involvement, that is, one's interest and motivation in a situation or in context, may take many forms. Involvement with a sport or team, with a musician or athlete, or with the event itself may be decidedly important to the success of the sponsorship. Involvement may be enduring and long-term or new and emerging, but in most instances it is thought to influence sponsorship message processing. An individual might have an overall interest, or domain involvement, in golf and this can in turn influence one's tendency to follow golf or a particular player and to identify with the sport (see Fisher & Wakefield 1998; Gwinner & Swanson 2003) and in this way become aware of sponsors.

Arousal or excitement similarly might encourage processing of sponsorship information if individuals are paying close attention to an event or activity and thus learning while viewing. Unfortunately, more is not necessarily better. At low to medium levels, involvement and arousal are both thought to support engagement and interest in a sponsored activity and outcomes related to sponsorship. As involvement and arousal become very high, individuals may be deeply focused on the activity at hand and therefore not able or willing to process sponsorship messages. Watching an exciting game may be so rousing that it limits attention to other things such as sponsors (Pham 1992). Of course, it is difficult to understand and predict how this works for any one individual.

Group factors might also influence how a person responds to sponsorship messages. In sports, one of the obvious considerations would be team allegiance. Companies value sponsorships because they feel that the energy and the loyalty found in sports may transfer to their brands. Evidence supports this possibility. For example, adults attending a collegiate football game were surveyed about their identification as a fan of the team and it was found that highly identified fans were more likely to know the sponsors of the team, and have positive attitudes and patronage behaviors toward them (Gwinner & Swanson 2003). Feelings of group membership cannot be simply picked up, however; to be most effective, the connection to the sponsor must seem genuine.

Further, there are "in-groups," where a person feels he or she is a part of the whole, and "out-groups," where a person feels excluded. These too play a role in response to sponsorship. Football (soccer) fans of the Stockholm team AIK transferred their on-the-field dislike of the rival Hammarby to dislike of the rival team's beer sponsor (Bergkvist 2012). This group factor might be particularly pronounced when considering products like beer or those with relatively low price and many alternatives (it might not be the case when evaluating a product like a laptop computer). Still, group allegiance is a key "antecedent" or important previously existing characteristic that influences many aspects of sponsorship information processing.

These individual and group factors only serve as examples. There may be many specific factors that would be important given the organization sponsoring, the event sponsored, and the particulars of the event. Managers should ask themselves, which considerations matter to our message or to outcomes we seek? Once individuals or group factors are identified as important, it is possible to predict behaviors and reactions in advance. For example, the Susan G. Komen Race for the Cure attracts a wide swath of participants in support of breast cancer research. There is, however, a difference between those actually having had cancer and those knowing someone having had cancer in terms of their commitment to an event and its sponsors (Cornwell & Coote 2005). For example, no matter how many other events a breast cancer survivor participates in, the findings suggest that they still identify with the Race for the Cure. It has special meaning for them.

Market factors

A slate of market factors could be listed for any sponsorship. Pre-existing levels of brand equity for brands and properties, communication clutter, and competitive activities are particularly influential. High-equity sponsors, those that are well-known brands, or household names have some advantages when communicating in sponsorship—as they do in other forms of advertising. A well-established brand does not have to work as hard to be associated with an event; in fact, a high-equity brand that fits well with a particular event (running shoe and running event) can be assumed or mistaken as sponsor even when having no formal association with the event. Low-equity and unknown brands must often communicate their brand name as well as their product category, and sponsorship's limited communication capabilities suggest collateral advertising may be needed.

The event attendees' experience of clutter, their perception that the environment has too many messages, negatively impacts their recall and recognition of sponsors (Cornwell et al. 2000). A study conducted in Russia and the United States considered the clutter on hockey team shirts and varied the number of logos (0, 2, and 12) (Kim et al. 2012). The findings showed that the cluttered shirt with 12 logos resulted in negative attitudes toward the team and an inability to correctly recall sponsors. Naturally, team presentation is a league decision for many US leagues, with the National Hockey League (NHL) having a logo-free approach while other leagues in Russia and Europe take a moderate or unrestrained approach to sponsor logos. The sponsorship manager does, however, have the ultimate judgment of what to sponsor and can decide if the value of being a shirt sponsor offsets the potential confusion created by clutter.

Competitive activities, both passive and active, play a key role in sponsorship communication. Communications by a direct competitor surrounding an event are typically considered to be ambushing and have the potential to detract attention from the true sponsor and confuse audiences. For example, Australia's GM Holden automaker flew its "Big Red" Holden blimp over its own sponsored V8 Supercar races but also cruised by places where it was not a sponsor, such as Toyota Stadium and Ford-sponsored cricket events. While the memory and attitude effects of sponsoring are still not fully understood, we know that the media attention surrounding clever ambushing creates a different context for communication. Managers typically cannot control market factors such as the competitive nature of an industry, a cluttered sponsorship roster for the event, or the aggressiveness of ambushers but they should be prepared to address issues as they arise.

Management factors

The role of management decisions on sponsorship outcomes may be critical to success. The choices managers make about their own policies can sometimes influence the policies of the event or venue. Given their knowledge of their products, and their own experience in sponsoring, they are often the ones who decide, for example, at what level they will sponsor (title, official partner), to what extent they will leverage or activate a sponsorship, and if they will partner with another brand for a joint promotion. They may establish policies that form the base of the communication platform. Research on sponsorship policy has found that corporate mission is often reflected in sponsorship policies regarding what a company will and will not sponsor (Cunningham et al. 2009). A sponsorship policy is a management instrument that can help align company mission and objectives with corporate communication tools such as sponsoring.

The money spent by a sponsor in addition to the contract that establishes the right to associate with a property is called leverage or activation. This spending is indispensable in building brand value from the sponsorship agreement (Cornwell 1995). In essence, it is up to the brand manager, and his/her budget, to determine the brand building possible from collateral advertising, promotions, and hospitality linked to a property sponsorship. As an example, EFG Bank, part of EFG International, headquartered in Switzerland, holds a large portfolio of sponsorships ranging from motorsport and dressage to classical and jazz music. Their approach to leveraging and activation is, however, in keeping with their private banking audience. For example, EFG's sponsorship of the Le Mans Classic motor race, where participating cars are previous Le Mans participants from 1923 to 1979, was leveraged by an advertisement in *Classic & Sport Car* magazine (Hancock 2013). While the event may have been an opportunity to network with high-wealth individuals, the advertisement, featuring a photo taken at the event, reached an additional audience that was not in attendance. For the event attendees, the advertisement served as a reminder of the experience and the brand. This ad was then featured on the blog page of the driver, samhancock. com, clearly in support of EFG.

Additionally, it should be noted that market and management factors might need to change during the course of the sponsorship contract. While it was not a sponsor, Oreo's instant advertising of its cookies during the blackout at the 2013 Super Bowl game is a testament to the potential of management to influence the moment. After confirming that the 34-minute blackout was only a loss of power with no injuries, Oreo published an ad via Twitter stating "You can still dunk in the dark" referring to dipping their cookies in milk when eating. "The ad—simple, surprising and instantly topical—became a viral hit, retweeted more than 15,000 times in the first 14 hours" (Farhi 2013). The ad served to build brand value and to make an uncomfortable situation amusing.

Processing mechanics

Having examined the three outside contributing factors, we now turn to the central box of Figure 4.1. The "processing mechanics" listed in this model take a communications perspective on sponsorship (i.e., they do not, for instance, seek to explain how hospitality at an event results in sales). Most sponsorships seek to develop attitudes and memory for the relationship between the sponsor and the sponsee. Memory is typically measured as recall or recognition of the sponsor brand and attitude or image as change that can be attributed to alignment with the sponsored activity or event. The following sections detail how the processing of sponsorship communications work. Note that these mechanics may work in combination.

Mere exposure

In the 1960s, social psychologist Robert Zajonc (1968) introduced the mere exposure hypothesis. Very simply, repeated exposure to a stimulus will develop a sense of liking in a person. Liking and even preference can be influenced by mere exposure. The potential for this to work in sponsorship is clear. Repeated exposure to a logo or brand icon, an advertising spokesperson, or the product itself can generate the mere exposure effect. Nivea, a German brand of skin products, signed a five-year deal with the Association of Volleyball Professionals tour which included changing the AVP's logo from yellow to the deep blue of Nivea's product packaging. "Their vision is to create a sea of blue at our events," stated the AVP CEO (Lefton 2010). One look from the sea, sky, or ground clearly identifies the Nivea brand and any event attendee will see the brand name repeatedly and in the preferred corporate blue of Nivea.

Low-level processing and reactivation

Another approach that seems to offer an easy path to communicating is low-level processing (Petty & Cacioppo 1981; Petty et al.1983). This posits that there is a central route to communication processing where we tend to think deeply about messages and arguments and, conversely, a second "peripheral" route where there is a low-level of processing that conserves effort but may still influence attitudes and ultimately behaviors. In practice, it is easy to see that this is more a continuum rather than a crisp distinction.

In low-level processing situations we may not be actively making choices or we may have attention focused elsewhere. For instance, when watching a musical performance by country and western singer Brad Paisley, we might be influenced to purchase products from his sponsor, Cracker Barrel Old

Country Store, due to his celebrity status, appealing music, or message creativity, or just about anything in the environment that is attached to the brand. Central route processing is less likely when there are no messages and arguments but only association, such as when Cracker Barrel places their iconic rocking chairs at an artist's meet-and-greet event or when a bus is wrapped in Cracker Barrel signage (Despres 2013).

Alternatively, something in the sponsorship context might reactivate memories a person holds for a time or for the particular brand. If the original experiences were positive, then reactivation can work like a mini-advertisement in a person's mind, building associations with the past or recovering them from memory. For example, the Citibank sponsorship of the Rolling Stones' "50 & Counting" tour is thought to touch all fans (Kirkpatrick 2013) but it can be imagined that the group's music will resonate strongly with those having grown up in the 1960s and 1970s. In this process, positive feelings surrounding the music of the past connect with the brand.

Matching/congruence

The most researched processing facilitator in sponsorship has been matching, which is the congruence or fit between the sponsor and the property. The idea here is that when things go together they are naturally easier to remember. It makes sense that a pet food company might sponsor a dog show or that a company that sells winter sports apparel sponsors a skiing competition. On the other hand, it could be that some degree of incongruence makes one "think twice" (a pet food company sponsoring skiing?) and, in doing so, a better memory for the relationship might result. Both types of processing are possible and when a brand is not a good match for sponsoring a particular event, then some incongruence is inescapable. This brings us to our next processing mechanic, articulation.

Articulation

If our goal is to establish a link between the sponsor and the sponsee, then we might need to tell a story that makes the link understandable. In experimental research, we find that even a single sentence making a meaningful connection between the event and the brand improved memory for the pair (Cornwell et al. 2006). Contrast these two sentences explaining why Nintendo sponsors the fictitious Indoor Fun Fest:

1. Nintendo officials stated "we hope this event is successful and at the end of the day the kids have had great indoor fun!"

2. Nintendo officials stated *"this sponsorship deal will highlight the fact that we provide kids with indoor fun."*

The last type of explanation supports memory because it articulates the relationship between the event and the brand. If these sorts of small changes to the wording of the explanation for a sponsorship make a difference in memory, one can imagine that a reasoned program of sponsorship plus leveraging and activation could support brand goals in sponsorship. Thus, instead of limiting relationships to those having a natural existing fit, we might create fit through our presentation of the sponsorship or through collateral advertising and promotion (also see Simmons & Becker-Olsen 2006).

Balance/meaning transfer

If we have a situation where instead of focusing on memory for the relationship, we want to focus on attitude or image, we might consider balance theory or meaning transfer. Balance theory (Heider 1958) explains that people like and seek consistent relationships, and when one is out of balance we seek to restore it. Applied to sponsorship, if you are indifferent to a brand or even have a negative attitude toward it, you might feel more positive if you learned that the brand was sponsoring an event you like. Research investigating the relationship between Food Lion retail grocery chain and the Special Olympics found that the well-liked event could influence favorable attitudes to the chain because it was a sponsor (Dean 2002). There is a cautionary note on this approach to transferring meaning. The relationship should be perceived as genuine, that the brand is not just borrowing a positive image. It is also important to believe the image of the sponsor can be changed; if not, meaning for the property could change instead. That is to say, in a person's attempt to restore balance, if the brand is well and truly hated, the sponsorship relationship might result in dislike or distain for the property.

Identification

In the case of sponsorship, identification is a feeling of sameness or oneness with regard to an event, team or organization, or the brand. Identification can be seen when people start to say "we" in an organization or group. We can readily see identification in sport when people feel that they are part of something. While identification might start in team identification and thus be more of an individual variable, it can also be created or supported by the event. In a study of sponsors for the Komen Race for the Cure running event, identification with the event resulted in purchase commitment toward the sponsors (Cornwell & Coote 2005). As with research in management on organizational identification, event participants developed identification through their tenure with the organization and through their feelings about the event's prestige.

Classical conditioning

The pairing of an event and a brand could be viewed as a type of classical conditioning where people learn over time from associations in their environment. For example, one's response to the Olympics might be a positive sense of pride, of hope, or of quality. If the Olympics (unconditioned stimulus) brings about these feelings naturally (unconditioned response) then if this were paired with something like the brand adidas, associations might build over time. The brand adidas (conditioned stimulus) after becoming associated with the Olympics might evoke feelings of pride or quality (conditioned response) on its own. It might be the case that people remember that a brand is an Olympic sponsor but it might also be the case that they now have a response to the brand that gives them a positive feeling of quality, and this may in turn influence purchase decisions.

Prominence heuristic

The idea of a prominence or market share advantage has long been recognized in advertising. Early research in advertising found that when given just a few seconds to view a print advertisement and see the visuals, but not long enough to consider all the writing, people often report that the advertisement was for a market leader or the brand with the largest share in the category. This tendency also influences how people process brands in sponsorship. It works even more powerfully if the brand is a market share leader and is related to the event in some logical or obvious way. For example, when we study signage in a baseball field, prominent and related non-sponsoring brands are more likely to be mistaken as sponsors than those less prominent and unrelated (Wakefield et al. 2007).

Relatedness partners neatly with prominence in the sense that individuals accredit a related sponsor over an unrelated sponsor with having been a supporter of an event. Given that hotdogs are *the* ubiquitous food at baseball games in the United States and a brand has capitalized on this relationship by naming their product for a baseball venue, wouldn't you think that "Ballpark Franks" was a sponsor of professional baseball rather than a firm such as the "Atlanta Bread Company" that sells loaves of bread?

Attribution theory

Attribution theory relates to the ways in which people explain events. In particular, it is concerned with the natural human desire to attach meaning to the behavior of others and to one's own behavior. As social psychologists Fiske & Taylor (1991) explain, "Attribution theory deals with how the social perceiver uses information to arrive at causal explanations for events." This aspect of information processing is particularly important when dealing with sponsorships that might be perceived as commercially minded. For example, in the sponsorship of charitable causes such as a half marathon to benefit AIDS awareness, if a sponsor in the men's hair care category were thought to be overly commercial in its communications, people may develop negative reactions to the sponsor. This attribution of "corporate self-interest" might then be related to negative attitudes (Dean 2002). Alternatively, if a sponsor is perceived to be genuine in its support of a cause, then positive attributions should result.

Clearly there are other ways in which sponsorship might work that are not only about how the message is processed. Some sponsorships are thought to be effective via feelings of reciprocity—give to my pastime and I'll buy from you (Pracejus 2004). When people know that the financial support of the sponsorship has made the activity they enjoy possible, they may buy from sponsors as a direct result. The National Association of Stock Car Racing (NASCAR) is thought to have many fans that buy sponsors' products because these firms sponsor the teams and drivers they love. Whether it is Goodyear automotive products or MillerCoors beer, "Nearly two-thirds of NASCAR fans are more likely to consider trying a company's product or service if that brand is an official sponsor of the sport" according to the results of the sixth annual NASCAR Sponsor Loyalty survey (Race Fans Continue to Embrace Engagement 2012).

Outcomes of sponsoring

Thinking

The final box of the model shown in Figure 4.1 considers cognitive (thinking), effective (liking), and behavioral outcomes from sponsorship. The main cognitive outcome for many sponsorships is awareness. This might be measured as brand recall or recognition (which might include non-sponsors as an added way to test the brand's impact by examining the "false positives"). Brands might also seek to develop an understanding of their product or service offering. For example, well-known skincare company, Nivea, sponsors sport with a particular goal of developing awareness for its newer men's product lines.

Liking

Effective response could include liking, preference, positive feelings, and improved attitudes. For some sponsors, the key goals are liking and preferences for the product or service. Having many brands within a category from which consumers might choose, can sponsorship provide that much of a difference in preference? Does knowing that vitamin and supplement retailer GNC sponsors March of Dimes mother and child health fundraising events make you like them that little bit more?

Through a number of different mechanisms sponsors might enhance image or attitude toward the brand. For others, especially at the corporate level, the real interest might be in positive reputation and feelings of goodwill toward the company. Charity and community-based sponsorships are often employed to elevate perceptions of the parent company while sport or music, as well as charity, might be utilized at the brand level.

Behaviors

Although the chain of response might be long and might move from awareness to understanding, liking, and then preference, most brands ultimately want to effect a change in consumer behavior through sponsorship. This might be measured by sales, but without careful tracking (and sometimes even with it) it is difficult to find the direct path from a sponsorship exposure to purchase. Alternatively, it might be useful to look at other interim behaviors such as loyalty card registration, positive word-of-mouth recommendations online, or responses to a trial offer.

The consumer-focused model of sponsorship-linked marketing was developed with consumer markets in mind. Much of the thinking also applies to business-to-business markets. Businesses will often utilize hospitality with suppliers, distributors, and prospects that they already know but they might still seek to build understanding of their product or service, as well as attitudes and eventual sales. In terms of behaviors they might consider business cards collected, follow up emails, or offers to bid for a project but the three outcomes are still essentially similar.

References

Amis, J. & Cornwell, T. B. (2005). *Global Sport Sponsorship*. New York: Berg.

Bergkvist, L. (2012). The Flipside of the Sponsorship Coin: Do You Still Buy the Beer When the Brewer Underwrites a Rival Team? *Journal of Advertising Research*, 52, 1, 65–73.

Cornwell, T. B. (1995). Sponsorship-linked Marketing Development. *Sport Marketing Quarterly*, 4, 4, 13–24.

Cornwell, T. B. & Coote, L. V. (2005). Corporate Sponsorship of a Cause: The Role of Identification in Purchase Intent. *Journal of Business Research*, *58*, 3, 268–76.

Cornwell, T. B., Relyea, G. E., Irwin, R. L. & Maignan, I. (2000). Understanding Long-Term Effects of Sports Sponsorship: Role of Experience, Involvement, Enthusiasm and Clutter. *International Journal of Sports Marketing and Sponsorship*, *2*, 2, 127–44.

Cornwell, T. B., Weeks, C. S. & Roy, D. P. (2005). Sponsorship-linked Marketing: Opening the Black Box. *Journal of Advertising*, *34*, 2, 21–42.

Cornwell, T. B., Humphreys, M. S., Maguire, A. M., Weeks, C. S. & Tellegen, C. L. (2006). Sponsorship-linked Marketing: The Role of Articulation in Memory. *Journal of Consumer Research*, *33*, 3, 312–21.

Cunningham, S., Cornwell, T. B. & Coote, L. (2009). Expressing Identity and Shaping Image: The Relationship between Corporate Mission and Corporate Sponsorship. *Journal of Sport Management*, *23*, 1, 65–86.

Dean, D. H. (2002). Associating the Corporation with a Charitable Event through Sponsorship: Measuring the Effects on Corporate Community Relations. *Journal of Advertising*, *31*, 3, 77–87.

Despres, T. (2013). Cracker Barrel Signs on as Brad Paisley Tour Sponsor. *Advertising Age*, February 28. Retrieved October 25, 2013 from http://adage.com/article/news/brad-paisley-s-tour-sponsored-cracker-barrel/240074/.

Farhi, P. (2013). Oreo's Tweeted Ad was Super Bowl Blackout's Big Winner. *The Washington Post*. Retrieved October 25, 2013 from http://articles.washington post.com/2013-02-04/lifestyle/36741262_1_ad-agency-ad-team-social-media.

Fisher, R. J. & Wakefield, K. (1998). Factors Leading to Group Identification: A Field Study of Winners and Losers. *Journal of Psychology & Marketing*, 15, 23–40.

Fiske, S. T. & Taylor, S. E. (1991). *Social Cognition*, 2nd edn. New York: McGraw-Hill.

Gwinner, K. & Swanson, S. R. (2003). A Model of Fan Identification: Antecedents and Sponsorship Outcomes. *Journal of Services Marketing*, *17*, 3, 275–94.

Han, S., Choi, J., Kim, H., Davis, J. A. & Lee, K.-Y. (2013). The Effectiveness of Image Congruence and the Moderating Effects of Sponsor Motive and Cheering Event Fit in Sponsorship. *International Journal of Advertising*, *32*, 2, 301–17.

Hancock, S. (2013). Good Example of Sponsorship Leveraging. Retrieved October 25, 2013 from http://samhancock.com/blog/2013/1/12/good-example-of-sponsorship-leverage.

Heider, F. (1958). *The Psychology of Interpersonal Relations*. New York: John Wiley.

Kholic (2013). Unique Baseball Cheering Culture in Korea. Retrieved October 24, 2013 from http://blog.kholic.com/4172/unique-baseball-cheering-culture-in-korea/.

Kirkpatrick, R. (2013). Citi's Rolling Stones Tour Sponsorship Touches All Fans. Retrieved October 25, 2013 from http://www.eventmarketer.com/article/citi-rolling-stones-tour-50#.UmrsOIJ6Oek.

Kim, K., Tootelian, D. H. & Mikhailitchenko, G. N. (2012). Exploring Saturation Levels for Sponsorship Logos on Professional Sports Shirts: A Cross-Cultural Study. *International Journal of Sports Marketing & Sponsorship*, January, 91–105.

Lefton, T. (2010,). Smooth Move: Nivea Signs Five-Year Deal to Title Sponsor AVP Tour. *Sports Business Daily*, March 31. Retrieved August 25, 2013 from http://www.sportsbusinessdaily.com/Daily/Issues/2010/03/Issue-138/Sponsorships-Advertising-Marketing/Smooth-Move-Nivea-Signs-Five-Year-Deal-To-Title-Sponsor-AVP-Tour.aspx.

Petty, R. E. & Cacioppo, J. T. (1981). *Attitudes and Persuasion: Classic and Contemporary Approaches.* Dubuque, IA: William C. Brown.

Petty, R. E., Cacioppo, J. T. & Schumann, D. (1983). Central and Peripheral Routes to Advertising Effectiveness: The Moderating Role of Involvement. *Journal of Consumer Research, 10,* 2, 135.

Pham, M. T. (1992). Effects of Involvement, Arousal, and Pleasure on the Recognition of Sponsorship Stimuli. *Advances in Consumer Research, 19,* 85–93.

Pracejus, J. W. (2004). Seven Psychological Mechanisms through which Sponsorship can Influence Consumers. In L. R. Kahle & C. Riley (eds), *Sports Marketing and the Psychology of Marketing Communications,* pp. 175–90. Mahwah, NJ: Lawrence Erlbaum Associates.

Race Fans Continue to Embrace Engagement (2012). *Sports Business Journal,* November 26. Retrieved October 25, 2013 from http://www.sportsbusiness daily.com/Journal/Issues/2012/11/26/Research-and-Ratings/NASCAR-Sponsor-Loyalty.aspx.

Simmons, C. J. & Becker-Olsen, K. L. (2006). Achieving Marketing Objectives through Social Sponsorships. *Journal of Marketing, 70,* 4, 154–69.

Wakefield, K. L., Becker-Olsen, K. L. & Cornwell, T. B. (2007). I Spy a Sponsor: The Effects of Sponsorship Level, Prominence, Relatedness and Cueing on Recall Accuracy. *Journal of Advertising, 36,* 4, 61–74.

Zajonc, R. B. (1968). Attitudinal Effects of Mere Exposure. *Journal of Personality and Social Psychology, 9,* 2, 1–27.

5

LEVERAGING AND ACTIVATION

The terms leverage and activation are often used interchangeably but over time have developed separate but related meanings. From a strategic perspective, if these are viewed as different undertakings it is essential to draw a distinction between them.

Sponsorship as "an investment, in cash or in kind, in an activity, person or event (sponsee), in return for access to the exploitable commercial potential associated with that activity, person or event by the investor (sponsor)" (Quester & Thompson 2001, p. 34) is the starting point. We turn now to what companies as sponsors do with their purchased access to potential. Sponsorship leveraging is the use of collateral marketing communications and activities to develop the marketing potential of the association between a sponsee and sponsor. It could include, but is not limited to, advertising, promotion, public relations, social media, sampling, direct marketing, internal marketing, hospitality, online, and business-to-business communications.

In a study of ten Olympic national sponsors for the Athens Olympic Games in 2004, seven categories of leveraging were identified for these sponsors: media advertising, sales promotions, publications, special events, new products/services, customer hospitality, and employee programs (Papadimitriou & Apostolopolou 2009). For example, a telecommunications consortium (OTE, COSMOTE, OTEnet) leveraged their Grand National Olympic sponsorship with an extensive advertising campaign featuring the message "One idea, one team, one voice." This same group developed a traveling multi-activity park where visitors experienced the Games atmosphere and the company's products. Some 500,000 visitors experienced the brand this way (Papadimitriou & Apostolopolou 2009). These two activities are very different and likely bring dissimilar brand values to the company.

Activational communications, or activation for short, can be viewed as a subset of sponsorship leverage. This idea of activation being a special subset of leveraging is a departure and a clarification that has strategic value. Activation can be described as "communications that promote the engagement, involvement, or participation of the sponsorship audience with the sponsor" (Weeks et al. 2008) and may include things such as event-related sweepstakes, event-driven mobile telephone competitions, and event-themed brand websites. In contrast, non-activational communications can be described as "communications that promote the sponsorship association, but that may be passively processed by the sponsorship audience." These may include communications such as on-site signage, sponsor name mentions, unidirectional online communications, and event-concurrent brand advertising.

In summary, the term *leverage* is used to describe all sponsorship-linked marketing communications and activities collateral to the sponsorship investment, while the term *activation* is reserved for those where the potential exists for audiences to interact and engage with the sponsor.

Why is the distinction important? Ideally a sponsorship manager would like to track leveraging investments and learn which are most valuable. If a clear distinction is made between the part of leverage that is deemed activation and the part that is not, then a better understanding of the value of these investments can be learned. As a case example, Cahill & Meenaghan (2013) documented the value of three consumer programs utilized by O2, the UK consumer phone service owned by Telefonica. The authors show the combined effects of a loyalty program called "Treats, where rewards are earned," their O2 venue sponsorship campaign program called "Priority Ticket" where tickets may be purchased in advance, and their rugby sponsorship activation called "Be the Difference," that engages fans. Participation in each of these three programs was found to reduce churn, or the departing of O2 customers to other telecommunications brands, by 10 to 19%. When, however, customers were engaged in more than one activity, churn was reduced from 18 to 28%. The Irish rugby team program "Be the Difference," although seasonal in nature, produced the lowest churn both alone, and in combination with other O2 activities. Although shorter in duration and with fewer overall participants, the "Be the Difference" program was clearly worth the investment and management could see this potential through separate measurement of marketing programs.

Leveraged activation

As noted by Weeks et al. (2008), it is possible that communications are activational for the attending event audience while non-activational for the mass–media audience (e.g., activities involving event attendees such as event-based competitions, product sampling, and merchandising). The mass–media audience might, however, find interest in well-orchestrated activations even if unable to participate. With this in mind, it may be useful to coin yet another term, "leveraged activation," for deliberate mass communications about event-based activations.

In this way, brands can document their brand activation and replay it to a mass audience. For example, Anheuser-Busch brand Bud Light is a multifaceted sponsor of the NFL (US National Football League). During the 2013 Super Bowl Anheuser-Busch re-branded a 200-suite hotel the "Bud Light Hotel." They built a temporary pedestrian bridge over a boulevard to a 3,500 capacity concert tent (Spera 2013). While the 20,000 Super Bowl attendees were immersed in the lifestyle-branding event, many more than could fit in the tent or the stadium were able to experience the activation by nightly video streaming on Myspace.com/BudLight. Following on the success of their previous hotels, in 2014 they needed a larger venue and so transformed a Norwegian Cruise Line Getaway ship into a floating hotel. Again, while there were only 3,000 "hotel" guests, there were many more thousands experiencing the story online.

The re-communication of event activation, without the opportunity to participate, is still one-way communication and does not have the same engagement potential as physical presence. It does, however, encourage the development of aspirational goals that include brand interaction, such as the belief that "if I ever go to the Super Bowl, I would like to see the Bud Light Hotel." It could encourage word-of-mouth referral and sharing of brand information in ways that function differently than traditional advertising. Alternatively, activation with mass participation might also be envisioned.

Why leverage?

A common belief with sponsorship is that one must leverage it with additional spending or the initial investment is likely wasted. There is good reason behind this notion, but it should never be blindly accepted. That is, there is no simple equation where more spending equals more success. What, therefore, are the central reasons to leverage a sponsorship?

Tell the brand story

Properties are ever more aware of the need to help the sponsor communicate in order to maintain a long-term relationship. That said, each property has a roster of sponsors and typically an arms-length, or outsider's view, of the sponsoring organization. If sponsors want to ensure their corporate or brand story is told, it will be primarily up to them and their intermediaries to leverage their investment.

Proctor & Gamble has been communicating their family orientation during the past several Olympic Games with the P&G Family Home. For the Vancouver Games, they rented a downtown office building for athlete families to hang out and relax.

> The Tide Laundry Center does laundry for free. The Pringles Zone has a bar serving nothing but Pringles chips in 29 flavors. The Pampers Village has diapers with the five Olympic rings imprinted on them and a play center for kids. There's even a salon for hairdos, makeovers and massages.
>
> *Berkes (2010)*

P&G furthered their storytelling at the 2012 Olympics in London when they combined this type of on-site leverage with a powerful "Proud sponsor of moms" advertising campaign. The message is emotional but consistent with the Olympic theme of the sacrifices required for excellence. In this way the brand tells its story though the sponsorship platform but also delivers to an at-home audience.

Leveraging as defense

Brands that are well-leveraged are less likely to be ambushed, or when ambushed, are more likely to be successful despite competition (Farrelly et al. 2005). Even in the face of extensive ambushing from the lesser-known Chinese sport brand Li Ning at the Beijing Olympics, official sponsor adidas was still thought to have gained "good value from its sponsorship investment" due to its own investment in leveraging (Pitt et al. 2010, p. 288).

Message variation and repetition

Message variation—having a theme, but also some variety—and repetition, support memory for a brand. Sponsorship agreements will inevitably include the opportunity to place logos and signage at an event or embed this information in programming. Sponsoring presents the opportunity for myriad unique forms of message repetition as the brand message or logo is experienced with various celebrities or attendees or during play, performance, and display. The repetition and variation is well beyond what might be achieved with traditional print or broadcast advertising.

While signage at an event is associated with greater sponsor recognition (Maxwell & Lough 2009), it is not the only way to gain sponsor awareness, nor is it always the best. Excessive signage, even if promised in an agreement and thus, in terms of leverage, without additional cost, may result in perceptions of commercialization. The turn toward commercialism is hotly debated in the context of college sports (McAlliser 2010). There are questions of the appropriateness of college sports as non-profits and their income under their special non-profit status (Wolverton 2009) but, moreover, if commercial messages are found where they are not expected, then excessive messaging can result in negative attitudes.

A study conducted in Germany considered attention paid to signage across the sports of soccer, handball, Formula One, and biathlon (Breuer & Rumpf 2012). Researchers utilized 26 film presentations of actual events and measured attention using eye tracking and post-tracking questions. The findings show that total time of the sign exposure, size, exclusiveness (amount of clutter from other sponsors), and placement of the sign all influence exposure impact in terms of recall. The researchers also note that saturation effects occur and that these truncate the recall probability. Finally, a pre-existing familiarity with the brand or being a brand consumer, increase recall.

Does being activational make a difference?

Weeks et al. (2008) demonstrated through an online experiment that leveraging involving active participation makes a difference in brand attitudes. The researchers were permitted to download web pages from the adidas site and to add fictional sponsorships, one for sport and one for music, with different types of participant engagement, activational or non-activational. Study participants clicking through to an activational page where they could explore information about competing athletes and their sports records, or performing bands and their musical history profiles displayed more favorable attitudes toward the sponsor adidas than when their final experience was to view non-activational "about us" company information.

Similarly, Degaris & West (2013) report that for a sample of NASCAR (National Association of Stock Car Auto Racing) fans, participating in sponsorship-linked sales promotions, such as games, contests, and sweepstakes, makes a difference in product consumption. In addition, thematically tied advertising and public relations were related to product consumption. It is difficult to know if self-selection bias might have influenced the results, since it might be the case that individuals that are frequent brand consumers might selectively perceive communications about the brand or want to be involved in contests where the product is given away as a prize. This is one of the common challenges of measuring integrated marketing communications. It is difficult to parcel out the effects of any one marketing program from those of others and from characteristics of consumers that lead them to respond variously.

Types of leveraging

Any collateral spending linked to a sponsorship could be considered leveraging. This section highlights the most discussed types. Leveraging related to social media, technology, and hospitality are of particular importance and in some cases, available research can guide decision-making. The challenge in each of these areas is to move from counting exposures or contacts to learning how the leveraging delivers brand value.

Social media

Social media in combination with sponsorship is a vast expanse of both risk and potential. We start with the definitions of *paid media* being awareness and public interest stemming from traditional advertising; *owned media* being the organization's branded and controlled media network in the community and online (e.g., websites); and *earned media* being word-of-mouth communication that is unpaid and not controlled. It is the latter that has generated enormous interest in recent years.

Interest in earned media stems from the potential cost effectiveness that peer-to-peer sharing brings the brand by doing the job of advertising, and doing it in a way that makes it seem less commercial. Word-of-mouth has been known for decades to be more persuasive than paid forms of communication (e.g., Herr et al. 1991) and electronic word-of-mouth has the same potential, especially when an individual feels that he or she is part of a virtual community online (Huang et al. 2012). Sponsorship is a natural ally to the development of earned media since earned media needs a starting point, something to talk about and share.

As a social media platform, Twitter has come to the fore in allowing individuals to develop personal brands (Pegoraro & Jinnah 2012). Viewing Twitter as a business tool has the effect that "athletes now communicate directly with fans and build up their own brand value, thereby making themselves more attractive to sponsors" (Pegoraro & Jinnah 2012, p. 89). Twitter is a natural complement to entertainment sponsorship where fans seek the inside scoop on how celebrities think and feel. It offers more immediacy to televised events (Bercovici 2013) and more opportunities for measurement.

There are potential drawbacks, however. A paramount risk in social media arises when existing groups such as music enthusiasts, festivalgoers, or fans are involved and have some established rapport within their community. The sponsoring brand must walk the tightrope between being a catalyst for conversation and sharing and being seen as appropriating grassroots initiatives.

Another possible risk of social media is that of social amplification. Just as positive images and attitudes can be promulgated, so can negative ones. In apprehension of a tweeting nightmare, the International Olympic Committee (IOC) developed social media blogging and Internet guidelines for the 2012 London Olympic Games. The guidelines were cast as being "better safe than sorry" by outlining exactly what athletes can and cannot do (Zmuda 2012). This measure of control over social media by the IOC met with backlash when athletes tweeted against Rule 40 that forbade their mention of sponsors in social media.

Technology-based leveraging

For large events, one technology-based option that is increasingly expected by attendees and participants is an event-specific mobile application. Mobile technology, when more than a static reference tool, offers the opportunity to engage with attendees and extend the contact time with these individuals beyond the event duration (Cartagine 2013). The 2013 Lollapalooza music festival app gave users band information and allowed them to create their own custom schedule (Lollapalooza.com 2013) but also functioned as an interactive connection for sponsors.

In sports, Heineken created a dual-screen app for the European Football Association's Champions League sponsorship. The Heineken app allowed casual betting with friends and was developed based on research showing that 72% of people watch the games at home and would value connectivity with friends during the game (Shields 2011). Naturally, functional, informational apps can also work with social media and other capabilities such as live streaming to make a one-stop shop for the event.

Hospitality

Sponsorship-related hospitality, also known as sponsorship-linked entertaining or corporate entertaining (Collett 2008), is primarily the hosting of business guests. The hosting and entertaining may be a prelude to business activities, a means of relationship maintenance, or a "thank you" for past business. A survey of the European Sponsorship Association found respondents rated entertaining core clients and stakeholders as high in importance, coming just after public visibility from brand image, awareness, and credibility (Day 2011).

Extensive documentation of the sponsor hospitality program at the 2000 Sydney Olympic Games and a survey of sponsors found that the preferential access that sponsors received resulted in new tourism networks for the country (Brown 2007). Brown (2007) explains that the 40,000 guests of Olympic sponsors, identified as visitors, were only a small portion of the corporate hospitality at the event. Importantly, these guests became both future visitors and future business partners.

When entertaining at sponsored events becomes too lavish, it might result in being viewed as bribery (Day 2011). While legislation varies from country to country, Day (2011) suggests following established corporate policy regarding bribery, documenting all expenditures, and matching the hospitality to the prestige of the event so that it is considered standard practice. In response to the UK Bribery Act that went into force in 2011, many previously accepted hospitality packages, such as those that come with Olympic sponsorship came under question. Many lamented the turn to conservative hospitality just before the London games:

> One Olympic sponsor who declined to be named says that when it signed up as a sponsor about three years ago it never envisaged having to phone up clients to ask if being its Olympic guest would pose a problem. The sponsor said the chance to showcase their association with the games to clients has been lost.
>
> *Blitz (2012)*

Leverage ratios

Most observers of sponsorship will agree that there are wasted opportunities when a contract is not backed by an additional investment; however, both the nature and extent of this additional investment can vary. Leverage ratios are defined as the amount spent on leveraging relative to the amount spent to engage in the sponsorship (also discussed as the sponsorship "deal"). The goal of a 1:1 ratio means that for every dollar or euro spent on the annual sponsorship contract, one dollar or euro should be spent on leveraging the relationship in the same year. Ratio rules of thumb range widely, as does actual spending. While it is informative to know what average leveraging figures are for an industry or type of sponsorship, spending in addition to the contract amount depends on several contextual factors.

1. *What is in the contract?*—Sponsorship "deals" or the agreed contract amount is the starting point for a leveraging ratio calculation but in comparisons across sponsorships and industries it is important to know what the contract includes. For example, if signage and advertising are inside one contract but an additional purchase for another then the comparison of leveraging ratios is potentially misleading. Comparison of contract amounts and leveraging is muddled if the base differs.

2. *What is counted as leverage?*—If sponsoring is integrated into marketing plans then elements that are "leveraging" in nature may be accounted for in other budgets. Thematically tied advertising would be one such example. If the firm were to pick up visuals or utilize sponsorship assets made available to them in the sponsorship contract, then this advertising would leverage the sponsorship but come from monies already budgeted for and accounted as advertising.

3. *Brand equities*—The brand equity of the sponsor and sponsee play into the amount needed for successful leveraging. Unknown brands and lesser-known properties typically must spend more than established brands and properties to build awareness or knowledge about who they are and what they do. Established brands may be simply reminding the marketplace to purchase. Brand recall is naturally supported by already established brand awareness and use (Breuer & Rumpf 2012).

4. *Duration of the relationship*—A sponsorship relationship that has been in place for many years may be more efficient to leverage. This may come with systems that are in place and people with background knowledge so that fewer mistakes are made and less training is needed. The target audience may only need reminding.

5. *Goals and objectives*—While it might seem obvious that the goals and objectives for the sponsorship will influence the leveraging, this is a strategic decision that hinges in part on the capabilities and experience of the marketing management and their aligned intermediaries. For example, sporting goods manufacturer Nike, with a mass communications goal and marketing capacity in place, can take a low-level sponsorship deal and leverage it multiple times the value of the deal to create a cost-effective advantage. In contrast, a firm might have a very low ratio if volunteer hours were the key leveraging contribution, as is the case with Habitat for Humanity, a charity that builds houses for people in need. Its corporate partners focus on community building and goodwill by involving company employees in the house building process. Even if employee hours away from work are counted in the cost of leveraging, they are still likely less expensive than advertising.

Collaboration in leveraging and activation

A final point about leveraging is that some of the best outcomes are collaborative. Relationships within the roster of sponsors for the property and all the associations those sponsors bring should be consider for their synergistic potential. For example, the New England Patriots football team brings its Facebook fans together for a "virtual tailgate" two hours prior to the game. In this pre-game time, Patriot fans interact, chat, and share tailgate party pictures (Feil 2012). JetBlue, a low-cost regional airline headquartered in New York, sponsors this virtual tailgate page. JetBlue also sponsors the Patriots cheerleader calendar shoot. Importantly, JetBlue is a codeshare partner of American Airlines, and American Airlines is a major corporate sponsor of the Patriots. Clearly, there is potential synergy and cost savings if complementary brands work together with the same property.

The mantra in business over the past decades has been to leverage sponsorship relationships more extensively. While it is true that the potential of many a sponsorship has been lost to a failure of leveraging and activation, it is not the leveraging ratio that matters but the connectivity and creativity of the link built between the sponsor and the sponsored. There is also unearthed potential in the synergistic combining of relationships that would move sponsoring toward taking advantage of its embedded networks.

References

Bercovici, J. (2013). Can Twitter Save TV? (And Can TV Save Twitter?). *Fortune*, October 28, 70–80.

Berkes, H. (2010). Olympic Sponsors Go for the Golden Image. *National Public Radio*, February 25. Retrieved September 15, 2013 from http://m.npr.org/news/Business/124068024?page=2.

Blitz, R. (2012). Corporates Turn Shy on Lavishing Sporting Hospitality. *Financial Times*. Retrieved April 2, 2014 from http://www.ft.com/cms/s/0/d07153d2-6c6b-11e1-bd0c-00144feab49a.html#axzz2xqGVW1jw.

Breuer, C. & Rumpf, C. (2012). The Viewer's Reception and Processing of Sponsorship Information in Sport Telecasts. *Journal of Sport Management*, 26, 521–31.

Brown, G. (2007). Sponsor Hospitality at the Olympic Games: An Analysis of the Implications for Tourism. *International Journal of Tourism Research*, 9, 315–27.

Cahill, J. & Meenaghan, T. (2013). Sponsorship at O2—"The Belief that Repaid." *Psychology & Marketing*, 30, 5, 431–43.

Cartagine, R. (2013). What Should Your Event App Do? *Meetings & Conventions*, 48, 3, 22.

Collett, P. (2008). Sponsorship-related Hospitality: Planning for Measurable Success. *Journal of Sponsorship*, 1, 3, 286–96.

Day, H. (2011). How to Avoid Sponsorship and Hospitality Becoming Forms of Bribery. *Journal of Sponsorship*, 4, 2, 100–4.

Degaris, L. & West, C. (2013). The Effects of Sponsorship Activation on the Sales of a Major Soft Drink Brand. *Journal of Brand Strategy*, 1, 4, 403–12.

Farrelly, F., Quester, P. & Greyser, S. (2005). Defending the Co-branding Benefits of Sponsorship B2B Partnerships: The Case of Ambush Marketing. *Journal of Advertising Research*, 45, 3, 339–48.

Feil, S. (2012). The Social Side of Sponsorship: Sports Marketers Take Aim at Activating Fan Engagement. *Adweek*, January 30. Retrieved October 25, 2013 from http://www.adweek.com/sa-article/social-side-sponsorship-137844.

Herr, P. M., Kardes, F. R. & Kim, J. (1991). Effects of Word-of-Mouth and Product-Attribute Information on Persuasion: An Accessibility-Diagnosticity Perspective. *Journal of Consumer Research, 17*, March, 454–62.

Huang, J., Hsiao, T. & Chen, Y. (2012). The Effects of Electronic Word of Mouth on Product Judgement and Choice: The Moderating Role of the Sense of Virtual Community. *Journal of Applied Social Psychology, 42*, 9, 2326–47.

Lollapalooza.com (2013). *The Official Mobile App.* Retrieved September 16, 2013 from http://www.lollapalooza.com/news-events/lolla-news/2013/07/03/the-official-mobile-app/.

Maxwell, H. & Lough, N. (2009). Signage vs. No Signage: An Analysis of Sponsorship Recognition in Women's College Basketball. *Sport Marketing Quarterly, 18*, 188–98.

McAlliser, M. P. (2010). Hypercommercialism, Televisuality, and the Changing Nature of College Sports Sponsorship. *American Behavioral Scientist, 53*, 10, 1476–91.

Papadimitriou, D. & Apostolopoulou, A. (2009). Olympic Sponsorship Activation and the Creation of Competitive Advantage. *Journal of Promotion Management, 15*, 90–117.

Pegoraro, A. & Jinnah, N. (2012). Tweet 'em and Reap 'em: The Impact of Professional Athletes' Use of Twitter on Concurrent and Potential Sponsorship Opportunities. *Journal of Brand Strategy, 1*, 1, 85–97.

Pitt, L., Parent, M., Berthon, P. & Steyn, P. G. (2010). Event Sponsorship and Ambush Marketing: Lessons from the Beijing Olympics. *Business Horizons, 53*, 281–90.

Quester, P. G. & Thompson, B. (2001). Advertising and Promotion Leverage on Arts Sponsorship Effectiveness (1998 Adelaide Festival of the Arts). *Journal of Advertising Research, 4*, 33–47.

Shields, R. (2011). Heineken Creates Dual-Screen App for Champion's League. *New Media Age, 28*, April, 3.

Spera, K. (2013). Super Bowl 2013 Corporate Branding, Concerts Coalesce at Bud Light Hotel. *The Times-Picayune.* Retrieved September 13, 2013 from http://www.nola.com/superbowl/index.ssf/2013/01/super_bowl_2013_corporate_bran.html.

Weeks, C. S., Cornwell, T. B. & Drennan, J. C. (2008). Leveraging Sponsorships on the Internet: Activation, Congruence, and Articulation. *Psychology & Marketing, 25*, 7, 637–54.

Wolverton, B. (2009). Commercialization in College Sports May Have "Crossed the Line" Congressional Report Says. *The Chronicle of Higher Education,* May 20. Retrieved November 24 from http://chronicle.com/article/Commercialization-in-College/47265.

Zmuda, N. (2012). The Social-media Strategy for Olympic Athletes: Better Safe Than Sorry. *Advertising Age, 83*, 28, 2–3.

6

ESTABLISHING SPONSORSHIP PORTFOLIOS

Visa, the financial services and payment products company, explains their global sponsorship portfolio this way:

> When the eyes of the world turn to marquee sporting and entertainment events, Visa is there. Our sponsorship of respected events brings the Visa brand to life and creates value for our stakeholders, amplifying our brand message, creating strong ties with consumers at moments of great passion and allowing Visa to deliver value to our clients and partners.
>
> *Visa Factsheet (n.d.)*

In their global portfolio, Visa sponsors FIFA World Cup soccer, the Olympic, and Paralympic Games. In the United States they hold a portfolio of sponsorships around the National Football League and a number of individual teams such as the Arizona Cardinals, Denver Broncos, and Minnesota Vikings. In Canada, they sponsor the International Film Festival and in the United Arab Emirates they sponsor the Dubai Shopping Festival. While the portfolio may address various consuming groups across regions, it should be in keeping with the brand's personality.

From the sponsoring brand perspective, a sponsorship portfolio has been defined as "the collection of brand and/or company sponsorships comprising sequential and/or simultaneous involvement with events, activities and individuals (usually in sport, art and charity) utilized to communicate with various audiences" (Chien et al. 2011).

A sponsorship portfolio is analogous to a media plan (Cornwell 1995). Both are set up to provide oversight and control over the process of promotion to external audiences. The more vested a company is in utilizing sponsorship, the more elements of media planning may be evident. In advertising, media planning is about the time and space allocated to the various media in a campaign, whereas in sponsorship the key elements of a sponsorship portfolio are time, space, and something more, called here sustentation.

Portfolio planning

Time

Sponsorship contracts are typically made for a set period: for example, a one-year sponsorship of the local under-11 soccer team or a 30-year contract to sponsor a stadium. Likewise, when a number of sponsorships are undertaken or held in a portfolio, they form an exposure pattern for the firm that resembles a media plan. Just as programs and publications in traditional planning have aspects of seasonality, so does sponsorship. Thoughtful sponsorship planning in a large portfolio should consider the temporal factors, such as attempting to balance sports in and out of season or the timing of international festivals in various locations.

Space

Space as a concept in sponsorship is as critical as it is in media planning, where space refers to the volume of advertising, or the size of a print advertisement in a newspaper. In sponsorship it might be a kiosk with a product demonstration, a background banner, or a foreground logo on a jersey. Strategic decisions about the type and extent of space needed are related to target audiences and objectives for the advertising campaign, and the same is true in sponsoring.

Cliffe & Motion (2005) documented the portfolio of Vodafone New Zealand mobile telecommunications. Vodafone's brand strategy has involved extensive sponsorship, including a portfolio that reflects their multiple audiences and brand objectives. Their portfolio at the time consisted of eight team sponsorships (e.g., New Zealand Silver Ferns Netball), four event sponsorships (e.g., Vodafone National Dragon Boating Festival), five individual sponsorships (e.g., snowboarder Deni Bevin), three media sponsorships, and community activities. The authors argued that a portfolio approach such as this allowed Vodafone "to achieve a range of brand objectives and adapt to changing strategic needs" (p. 1075).

Sustentation

The media planning analogy is useful, but rather than a set of purchases the sponsorship portfolio is a set of relationships. These relationships must be sustained, nurtured, or perhaps ended but they do not function like a media buy. The term "sustentation" is utilized here to reflect need for financial support but also sustaining the life of the relationship through interaction and communication. In media planning there is adjustment annually, or if needed more frequently, to the plan of exposures for a brand—an unpopular program is dropped, a new blog is added. Maintenance of a portfolio of sponsorship agreements requires periodic pruning or extension as well. These are, however, relationships, some with contracts that would be difficult to dissolve, but more importantly, they come with some level of commitment to a partnership.

For some sports, it has been shown that winning makes a difference in the way in which the marketplace values a sponsorship (Cornwell et al. 2001). There is the temptation to drop a losing team or end a relationship with a critically reviewed music tour, but savvy sponsors often stick with their properties through difficult times. Cahill & Meenaghan (2013) report that the Irish O2 telecommunications firm has sponsorship portfolio philosophies titled "You've got to be in it for the long haul" and "If you're in it for winning, it's going to be a short relationship" to reflect the need for long-term relationships in rugby that go beyond on-field performance. Their thinking in rugby applies broadly to all kinds of sponsorships.

There are aspects of sponsorships besides performance that do merit adjustment of a portfolio. A classic example of adjustment for non-performance issues would be the comment by British PGA Tour golfer, Paul Casey. In the context of the Ryder Cup, he commented that he "properly hates Americans" and this led to end of his Titleist (US brand golf ball) sponsorship (Carter 2004). Titleist subsequently released a statement noting that: "First and foremost we want people to understand that Mr. Casey's comments do not reflect the views of the Acushnet Company and were not made in his capacity as an endorser of our products" (Carter 2004). In less dramatic ways, the brand objectives of the firm or the brand assets of the property may change or become incompatible. The loss of a key performer or player can make a difference to the property's drawing power.

It is also the case that brands have to make adjustments to portfolios to match their markets and their budget. Kodak, one-time dominating global brand in the photographic equipment category, and 20-year sponsor of the Olympics, cited a shift to digital and a "shift in marketing tactics" when it exited Olympic sponsoring after the Beijing games (Paul 2007). Although a change in tactics was the stated reason for the change, the cost of sponsoring was too much for a firm that would file for bankruptcy in 2012.

The analogy to media planning breaks down even further when one considers human resources. People, either from within the firm or hired from a third party, typically must continually manage aspects of engagement between the firm and the property. Unlike the media campaign that is off the desk of the planner near the time of execution, a sponsored event requires greater commitment as it approaches. In fact, the human resources commitment surrounding activation of sponsorship is often underestimated. For this reason, the term "sustentation," with the meaning of maintenance of activity and sustaining relationships is descriptive of both the "means and funds" that keep sponsorships in the portfolio viable.

Building brand associations

Traditional advertising is used to build brand associations (Keller 1993), everything connected to the brand in memory, good and bad, old and new. An interesting aspect of building brand associations is that connections that are weak or seemingly inconsequential may be utilized creatively to support memory for the sponsor–event relationship.

How sponsorship information is remembered and later retrieved depends on the exposure and the receiver (Cornwell 2008). Past research finds that the knowledge a person holds about a sport influences his or her perception of the congruence of a sponsor–event pairing (Roy & Cornwell 2004). Similarly, the knowledge a person holds about a celebrity musician may influence his or her feelings that they match well with a sponsor. The pairing of a brand or a corporate name with an event or activity presents the opportunity to borrow from the stores of knowledge that people already have.

Research in psychology shows that when recall is cued with an associate of a to-be-remembered word, the network of associations emanating from both the cue and the target are involved in the recall process (Nelson & McEvoy 2002; Nelson et al. 1997). This suggests that if we know a little about the past of the brand and those things it might sponsor, it is possible to make predictions about what kinds of combinations might support memory. Importantly, this can go beyond the obvious primary associations (both entities being from the same city), to subtle secondary or tertiary associations that two or more entities share that could bind them together in memory. For example, the Mastercard credit card corporate logo shows connecting circles. These circles can become any type of ball, such as a golf ball or baseball, in a sport sponsorship communication.

Portfolio effects

In order to examine the effects of the combining of properties in a portfolio in a controlled way, experiments are helpful. Sponsorship portfolios can be complex but the vast majority of research examines how a single sponsorship works, not how a set of sponsorships work in combination. If combining two properties together could be tracked by monitoring some traceable characteristic, it could inform the ways portfolios are developed.

Researchers in examining portfolio effects (Chien et al. 2011), started by selecting fictitious brands (in order to have a neutral starting point). Five brand personality dimensions were measured for numerous sport and charity properties: sincerity, excitement, competence, sophistication, and ruggedness (based on Aaker 1997). Then sport and charity properties were combined in a two-property portfolio that had particular brand personality characteristics such as ruggedness and sophistication. There was also interest in the order in which one adds a property to a portfolio. The hypothesis was that the first property would frame thinking about the second one.

In the experiments, study participants read a newsletter that communicated information about the sponsorships. Findings showed that properties combined in a portfolio could make a difference to brand meaning and brand clarity. For example, combining a rugged sport such as rugby with a charity like Greenpeace, known for its Rainbow Warrior fleet of ships, gave a boost to perceptions of ruggedness (see Figure 6.1). The combining of the Rugby World Cup and Greenpeace results in a "spiky pattern" that emphasizes ruggedness (but not sophistication) whereas the combination of the Professional Golf Association (PGA) and the National Basketball Association (NBA) results in a mixed, offsetting pattern without a strong in-tandem spike on any brand personality dimension. Portfolios with this type of pattern do not communicate powerfully on any particular brand personality characteristic.

Additionally, findings showed that sport is a more flexible frame for subsequent sponsorships than charity. That is, sponsorship of sport seems to allow for charity to follow whereas sponsorship of charity may be more conceptually narrow and one may have to work harder to achieve clarity and consistency when a brand is first presented as a charity sponsor. Although evidence is limited, the logic is sound: when a broad encompassing image is developed first, it is easier to become specific, but the reverse may not be true.

The most important finding from this work is that to make an individual characteristic stand out from the combined portfolio, it may be useful to think not of high performance on all characteristics but rather to seek portfolio elements with spikes or high ratings on those most desired. Similarly, mixed elements in a portfolio, some sophisticated, some not, some sincere, and some not, can hurt brand clarity. The possibility is that countervailing rankings across characteristics—we used brand personality characteristics, but any image element could be used—may turn to perceptual soup.

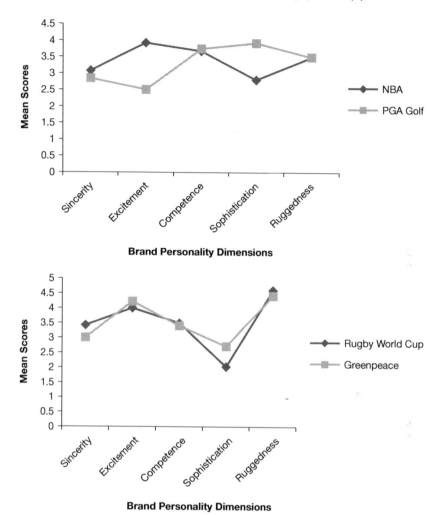

FIGURE 6.1 Brand personality portfolio effects

Source: Adapted from Chien et al. (2011).

Brand pillars

A strategic tool that works well with sponsorship portfolios is the idea of selecting and maintaining brand pillars. Brand pillars are central brand attributes (Mizik & Jacobson 2008). Marketing managers utilize this thinking both at a general level such as Young & Rubicam's Brand Asset Valuator model, including differentiation, relevance, esteem, knowledge, and energy elements (Mizik & Jacobson 2008), or at a specific level. For example, in building a sponsorship portfolio, a brand such as Mercedes-Benz holds a portfolio of sport, fashion, and community associations. All sponsorship pillars connect with their brand orientation to luxury, innovation, and design. Their global sponsorship of Fashion Week is just as consistent with their brand as their sponsorships of Formula One auto racing, golf, polo, and soccer. Their portfolio is balanced across sponsorships in art, sports, and community support and all connect to their brand pillars.

Other portfolio concerns

Pre-existing relationships

Many sports properties come with a beneficiary–sponsorship relationship. The sport has a charity partner with which they work and when one sponsors the sport, one indirectly (or directly) sponsors the charity. For example, the US National Football League has held a beneficiary sponsorship with the American Cancer Society and its NFL Play 60 program, which encourages 60 minutes of active play for children per day.

Perhaps one of the most notable relationships has been that of the children's charity UNICEF with European soccer clubs. UNICEF held a unique position with Futbol Club Barcelona from 2006 to 2010 where the team donated 1.5 million euros per year to UNICEF and wore the UNICEF logo on their shirts. That is to say, in this instance, the sport property sponsored the charity. Barcelona upended this relationship in 2010 when they accepted a 150 million euro, five-year agreement with the Qatar Foundation, another charity focusing on education, research, and community development.

Both current and past beneficiary–sponsor relationships come with a pre-existing set of associations with the property. If these associations are known and well understood they might be something that a brand manager might capitalize on and build. Important in building a portfolio is to understand the available building blocks of meaning and memory and these may come from beneficiary–sponsorship relationships.

Event roster or property portfolio

From the sponsor perspective, you are in some instances the title sponsor, but most often, you are one among many that a property holds. Perhaps you are an "official sponsor" of a product category such as the official telecommunications company, or maybe an official supplier. For a particular event your brand is associated with the other brands on the "event roster." This roster, although not part of the sponsoring firm's portfolio, may influence how any individual sponsor is perceived.

The sheer number of sponsors can also impact the response to the sponsorship. For example, as the number of sponsors increases so does the perception that there is some sales or commercial motive behind the sponsorship (Ruth

& Simonin 2006). Further, research considering the logos on hockey player shirts shows reduced brand recall for shirts with high levels of advertising intensity (Mikhailitchenko et al. 2012).

Groza et al. (2012) showed that there is a dynamic portfolio effect on perceptions of the sponsored organization's brand equity. Their thinking is based on the role of congruence and the possibility that one incongruent contributor to the portfolio can influence overall perceptions of the property. They found varying results depending on whether the incongruent sponsor held a more or less important (title sponsor or presenting sponsor) role and also depending on the number of sponsors involved. Importantly, an incongruent title sponsor was damaging to the property's brand equity perceptions.

Strategically, this incongruence outcome can be precluded if the anchor or title sponsor comes first and congruent sponsors follow on the property's roster. For example, the Mercedes-Benz Arena in Shanghai has the potential to attract other luxury brands in a bid for synergy while the Levi's Stadium in San Francisco would work well with other lifestyle brands. In both instances, the brand awareness of the naming rights sponsor is advantageous to the venues being sponsored and to their potential to build a coherent roster of sponsors.

This finding gives further support to the notion that it is in the brand's best interest to learn as much as possible about the other sponsors that will be on the property's roster. There might be reasons to work with a property to build their roster. A brand might bring in other partners with which they have worked. Perhaps more importantly, it could be possible to build meaningful alliances that support awareness, image, or product distribution.

Celebrity endorsement portfolios

Similar to event roster effects, there is also the likelihood of celebrity endorser effects that stem from an individual's set of relationships. Researchers Kelting & Rice (2013) examined consumer memory for celebrity advertising under conditions where a single celebrity advertises for more than one brand. Their findings show that the brands in a celebrity endorsement portfolio can interact with one another and either reduce or enhance recall and attitude depending on how they match the celebrity and the type of measure utilized. Their work only examined one endorser brand, soccer superstar David Beckham, and found that powerfully good or poor brand matches in a celebrity portfolio can overshadow responses to moderately matched brands in terms of recall.

Portfolio and roster analysis is only just beginning to develop in earnest. The complex and layered nature of these effects makes them puzzling to predict and challenging to analyze. Attention to them is worthwhile though since it is already possible to see that they can have powerful influence on sponsorship outcomes.

References

Aaker, J. L. (1997). Dimensions of Brand Personality. *Journal of Marketing Research*, *34*, 3, 347–56.

Cahill, J. & Meenaghan, T. (2013). Sponsorship at O2—"The Belief that Repaid." *Psychology & Marketing*, *30*, 5, 431–43.

Carter, I. (2004). Casey Loses Sponsor and Lead. *The Observer*, November 21. Retrieved on November 25, 2013 from http://www.theguardian.com/sport/2004/nov/21/golf.theobserver.

Chien, M., Cornwell, T. B. & Pappu, R. (2011). Sponsorship Portfolio as Brand Image Creation Strategy. *Journal of Business Research*, *64*, 142–49.

Cliffe, S. & Motion, J. (2005). Building Contemporary Brands: A Sponsorship-based Strategy. *Journal of Business Research*, *58*, 1068–77.

Cornwell, T. B. (1995). Sponsorship-linked Marketing Development. *Sport Marketing Quarterly*, *4*, 4, 13–24.

Cornwell, T. B. (2008). State of the Art and Science in Sponsorship-linked Marketing. *Journal of Advertising*, *37*, 3, 41–55.

Cornwell, T. B., Pruitt, S. W. & Van Ness, R. (2001). An Exploratory Analysis of the Value of Winning in Motorsports: Sponsorship-linked Marketing and Shareholder Wealth. *Journal of Advertising Research*, *41*, 1, 17–31.

Groza, M. D., Cobbs, J. & Schaefers, T. (2012). Managing a Sponsored Brand: The Importance of Sponsorship Portfolio Congruence. *International Journal of Advertising*, *31*, 1, 63–84.

Keller, K. L. (1993). Conceptualizing, Measuring, and Managing Customer-based Brand Equity. *Journal of Marketing*, *57*, 1, 1–22.

Kelting, K. & Rice, D. H. (2013). Should We Hire David Beckham to Endorse Our Brand? Contextual Interference and Consumer Memory for Brands in a Celebrity's Endorsement Portfolio. *Psychology & Marketing*, *30*, 7, 602–13.

Mikhailitchenko, A. G., Tootelian, D. H. & Mikhailitchenko, G. N. (2012). Exploring Saturation Levels for Sponsorship Logos on Professional Sports Shirts: A Cross-cultural Study. *International Journal of Sports Marketing & Sponsorship*, *13*, 4, 267–81.

Mizik, N. & Jacobson, R. (2008). The Financial Value Impact of Perceptual Brand Attributes. *Journal of Marketing Research*, *45*, February, 15–32.

Nelson, D. L. & McEvoy, C. L. (2002). How Can the Same Type of Prior Knowledge Both Help and Hinder Recall? *Journal of Memory and Language*, *46*, 3, 652–63.

Nelson, D. L., Bennett, D. J. & Leibert, T. W. (1997). One Step Is Not Enough: Making Better Use of Association Norms to Predict Cued Recall. *Memory and Cognition*, *25*, 6, 785–96.

Paul, F. (2007). Kodak to End Olympic Sponsorship after 2008 Games. *Reuters*. Retrieved November 25, 2013 from http://www.reuters.com/article/2007/10/12/us-kodak-olympics-idUSWEN164520071012.

Roy, D. P. & Cornwell, T. B. (2004). The Effects of Consumer Knowledge on Responses to Event Sponsorships. *Psychology & Marketing*, *21*, 3, 185–207.

Ruth, J. A. & Simonin, B. L. (2006). The Power of Numbers: Investigating the Impact of Event Roster Size in Consumer Response to Sponsorship. *Journal of Advertising*, *35*, 4, 7–20.

Visa Factsheet (n.d.). *Visa Global Sponsorship Portfolio*. Retrieved October 25, 2013 from http://corporate.visa.com/_media/fifa-media-kit/Global-Sponsorship-Portfolio.pdf.

7

MEASURING SPONSORSHIP OUTCOMES

Measurement approaches in sponsorship could be broadly grouped as either taking a public relations approach characterized by capturing and summarizing outputs from sponsorship—number of brand mentions, audience logo impressions, social media fans and followers, and the nature of these outcomes (e.g., positive, negative), or an advertising and marketing approach. The advertising and marketing approach is typically survey-based and is concerned with attitudes developed due to sponsorship, memory for the sponsor, image changes, and purchase intentions. The final form of research reports can range from descriptive statistics to sophisticated causal modeling. While there is also a place for qualitative and exploratory research in sponsorship, less of it is found.

Sponsorship measurement comes from commercial suppliers offering measurement and evaluation services, property-developed research, brand-developed research, or some combination. Brands already accustomed to seeking evidence for managerial decision-making have developed or extended measurement instruments to capture sponsorship impacts. At the same time properties have learned that sponsorship sales are supported by data, and they have begun to invest in systematic measurement. The number of commercial suppliers to the sponsorship industry has grown dramatically over the past decade, including start-up companies and traditional suppliers of advertising research who have developed a specialization in sponsorship.

One of the earliest commercial suppliers of measurement to the sponsorship industry was Joyce Julius & Associates from Ann Arbor, Michigan. The company began in 1985 by supplying information to sponsors on the amount of time that their logo was visible during a sponsored event. One of their major clients was and continues to be the auto racing industry. This information on exposure time was combined with information on the cost of advertising during the same broadcast to arrive at an advertising equivalency measure of impact. While the approach has been criticized for equating (in financial terms) intermittent logos and focused advertising messages, it was an early yardstick in an industry with a real need for analytics (Cornwell 1995).

Joyce Julius has evolved their technique over the decades. They are now able to master all sorts of media- and event-based sponsorship activities and take into account brand communication, size and location, brand clutter, and even the extent to which the sponsor brand information is in clear focus (Joyce Julius & Associates 2013). For example, in the 2013 NASCAR Sprint Cup Series, Jimmie Johnson's 47 sponsors received 95 mentions and 14 hours, 32 minutes and 31 seconds of exposure time that was valued at $55 million (Karp 2013). There is evidence that advertising equivalency figures in sponsorship are inflated (Crompton 2004) yet they persist in use. Why?

Although advertising equivalency measures now capture more advanced aspects of logo exposure, they are still not the same as advertising. You can, however, at least compare last year's exposure to this year's and your exposure to that of your major competitor. In short, advertising equivalency measures remain popular in the sponsorship industry for benchmarking purposes. In an industry struggling with the challenges of measurement in a loose dynamic environment, and with managerial pressures on accountability issues, even relative measures are welcome.

Unfortunately, two problems draw the value of advertising equivalency measures into question. First, brand managers know that these metrics tend to be inflated in terms of their worth relative to advertising, and they thus apply their own discounting method to received reports. Even savvy property managers will discount their own report to current and potential sponsors to avoid overstating their value. Second, managers on both sides of the relationship that do not apply a discount are likely not communicating sincerely with those in an organization that might take the numbers at face value. In sum, this public relations-style measure is useful but limited; therefore, many sponsors and properties measure their sponsorships in other ways.

Managerial perspectives on measuring

Whether a brand or property employs a commercial supplier or develops measurement on its own, it is important to consider the management process as well as the measurement itself. In a thoughtful piece about the "seven deadly sins of performance management," Michael Hammer, president of a management education firm, argues that operational measurement is fundamental and of increasing importance to strategic systems that guide decision-making (2007). That is to say, in sponsorship, particular outcome measures flow into evaluative systems or summative dashboards. But if these individual measures of short-term outcomes are not meaningful then larger evaluative models built on them are compromised. Reports having numbers are, however, considered quantified and may appear convincing. As Hammer explains, his seven measurement sins include:

1. *Vanity*—the selection of measures that make management look good.
2. *Provincialism*—keeping within organizational or industry boundaries when new measures are needed.
3. *Narcissism*—measuring from one's own point of view, not that of the customer.
4. *Laziness*—assuming one knows what to measure without giving it thought.
5. *Pettiness*—measuring a small subset of what should be measured.
6. *Inanity*—measuring without thought of how measurement or actions based on it will influence the organization.
7. *Frivolity*—not being serious about measuring.

All these shortcomings in measurement can be found to some degree in sponsoring, but vanity and provincialism are the standout vices. In sponsoring, it is easy to make a well-established brand look good. Brands that have a natural link to a property are likely to begin with awareness that can be further built by sponsorships. In these situations, "prominence bias,"—the tendency of a well-known brand to be presumed to be a sponsor, in combination with a "relatedness bias,"—the tendency of a related brand to be presumed to be a sponsor through their relation to the activity, have been shown to influence outcome measures consistently (Johar & Pham 1999). This means that established, property-matching brands would be presumed to be sponsors when consumers are asked a recall question, even if they were not present in any way.

Double vanity (it makes you look good and well liked) can also be found in sponsorship-linked social media. Here, having high traffic and ever increasing "likes" may seem compelling and satisfying but may not translate to meaningful changes to targeted behaviors like trial, purchasing, or donating. High traffic and likability need to be coupled with other measures to be truly meaningful. This is even more troublesome if brands "buy likes" through couponing or other means.

Historically bounded or provincial measurement in sponsorship stems partly from the measurement that is often packaged in the sponsorship deal coming from the property. For example, an annual survey of symphony orchestra season ticket holders or golf tour fans may be included in the sponsorship deal and may provide valuable insights and a longitudinal look at loyalty or sponsorship-linked purchase commitment. It may, however, further lock in the types of measurement undertaken. First, to depart from the already collected information means a break in comparability unless the previous measures are retained and new ones are added. This might result in an overly long data collection instrument. Further, if sponsors want specific, perhaps more meaningful measurement for their brand, this may be an issue if the property feels they cannot afford additional brand-specific measurement, for one, if not all, sponsoring brands. Breaking with the past can be effortful.

Sponsorship has a few sins that might be added to Hammer's list. First would be the sin of neglect. In arguing for broad range measurement in sponsorship, scholar Tony Meenaghan (2011) points to international survey research on measurement and concludes, "two-thirds of sponsors do not 'always or almost always' measure sponsorship effectiveness." Indeed, a telling statistic from the 102 respondents to the 2010 ANA/IEG Survey of Sponsorship and Events Measurement is that "Among those firms that have a dedicated budget for measuring the results of their sponsorship initiatives, on average, the budget is equivalent to 2.3% of the dollars spent to acquire sponsorship rights" (Association of National Advertisers and International Events Group 2010, p. 10). Importantly, only 38 of 102 respondents *had* a dedicated budget.

Oddly enough, alongside the penchant not to measure sponsorship outcomes, there is also a tendency toward a certain type of gluttony. When measurement is undertaken, and especially when it comes as part of a property's annual survey (such as the season ticket holders as mentioned), then there can be an excess of measurement to the point of waste. While the property may be proud to offer the findings from over 10,000 season ticket holders, statistically, this number of respondents is likely not needed. Moreover, these may not be the most valuable patrons to shed light on questions of sponsorship success. A better mix of respondents might include single-ticket purchasers or those who did not attend but were aware of the event or those who watched part of the broadcast of the event.

Sponsorship impact

The predominant orientation in measuring sponsorship outcomes has focused on consumers of the sponsor's product or service. For this reason, we know more about measurement in this area. There is, however, a growing interest in measuring sponsorship outcomes for business-to-business relationships in sponsoring. Also, with the growth of modeling in sponsorship analytics, there is a developing interest in measuring interim changes in processes and impacts to marketing assets.

Sponsorship impact on individuals as consumers

Typical consumer, viewer, or attendee outcomes can be grouped into cognitive, effective, and behavioral categories (Cornwell et al. 2005). Common cognitive outcomes are recall and recognition of the sponsor. Effective outcomes include liking, change in attitude, and product or service preference. Behavior outcomes of sponsorship are wide-ranging and could include purchase, renewal of a contract, donation, recommendation to a friend, or product trial. It is, however, not behavior but usually behavioral *intention* that is measured in most sponsorship research both in lab experiments and in the field (Cornwell et al. 2005).

When considering measures for sponsorship, it is useful to return to the customer measures at the core of marketing. One framework (adopted from Ambler et al. 2002) describes five customer impacts from marketing: brand awareness, brand associations, brand attitudes, brand attachment, and brand experience. These five consumer impacts of marketing are summarized here, noting their relevance to sponsorship.

Brand awareness

Defined as the extent and ease to which customers recall and recognize the brand and can identify the products and services with which it is associated.

Sponsorship can contribute to brand awareness and is one of the most frequently noted objectives for sponsoring. Brand managers want to know if individuals, subsequent to the sponsorship program, are better able to identify the brand. That said, there is also a strong interest in understanding the awareness, on the part of individuals, of the sponsor–property relationship. There are several values to sponsorship relationship awareness: (1) it can support feelings of reciprocity when the support from the sponsor is understood; (2) it may be important in image building—that individuals are aware of the relationship (e.g., in charity sponsorship); (3) it can serve as a measure of brand awareness linked to this communication approach and thus inform managers; and (4) sponsor relationship awareness can inform the sponsor about competitive activity such as the success of ambushing.

It is also the case that sponsorship could be measured as a contributor to brand awareness directly without consideration of the property sponsored. Brand awareness in sponsorship is typically captured with aided recall, also known as recognition. Aided recall can take many forms, such as cueing with the sponsor for the event or with the event for the sponsor (Cornwell et al. 2006). Cued recall could also use the brand category "When you think of [Category Y, e.g., banks] what sponsorships come to mind?" (Tripodi et al. 2003).

Less often, surveys are utilized to measure free recall, or unaided awareness. For instance, researchers in Austria (Grohs et al. 2004) asked "Which sponsor of the Alpine Ski World Championships 2001 in St. Anton do you recall?" In another example of free recall measurement, jazz festival attendees were asked to identify any festival sponsors (Oakes 2003).

Recognition is typically measured by giving individuals a list of possible sponsors and asking whether or not each brand was or was not a sponsor. In many recognition studies foils or non-sponsoring brands are included to check on the accuracy of people's recognition (see for example, Johar et al. 2006). But the use of these foils, typically popular and well-known brands in the same category as the sponsor, can also lead to misperceptions. A lesser-known brand or a business-to-business brand as a true sponsor may not fare well against well-known foils because they are related to the event and seem like a logical choice. The unfamiliar brand might have been very successful via sponsoring when measured against its starting base of awareness, but the comparison to a strong foil makes it look bad.

Brand associations

Defined as the strength, favorability, and uniqueness of perceived attributes and benefits for the brand and firm.

Sponsorship is often measured in terms of its ability to develop, change, or improve brand image. The essence of a developed brand image in the mind of an individual is the composite of various types of favorable, strong, and unique brand associations (Keller 1993).

Sponsorships can help build brand associations. Investec is a financial asset management company that invests in England's cricket test matches. During the summer of the 2013 Ashes event, the highest profile match in all of the sport, social media mentions of the Investec brand were predominantly related to the event. From the start of July to mid-September, 58% of social media mentions of Investec related to the Ashes, 12% to Super Rugby (another sponsorship), and 30% to investments and non-sport topics (Whitney 2013). In this way Investec built associations to a well-regarded event and potentially to the positive associations of the event.

Associations between a brand and a property could develop organically over time or they could be actively managed. If hoping to develop unique,

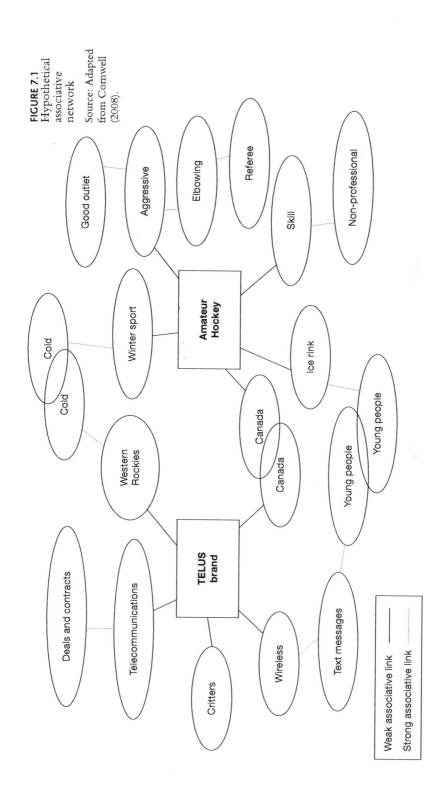

FIGURE 7.1
Hypothetical
associative
network

Source: Adapted
from Cornwell
(2008).

inimitable associations, it is up to the sponsor and property to choose those associations that are most beneficial. For instance, Figure 7.1 shows the hypothetical associative network between Canadian telecommunications brand TELUS and amateur hockey. The TELUS brand could seek to develop the association to hockey around young people or their Canadian heritage where there are already overlapping associations. Overlapping associations provide a base from which to build—even though telecommunications and hockey arrive at youth differently, this shared concept does not need to be established.

In contrast, the telecommunications company has no natural association to "critters" but has a long-standing image platform built around animals and wildlife that includes a partnership with the World Wildlife Fund. They also have a partner in the Canadian Football League. In combining their available unique associations, TELUS featured a panda with a football as a visual in their contest "What's your favorite #greycupmemory?" This activation around the Grey Cup Championship was uniquely theirs in that few brands could legitimately combine these disparate images.

As with many aspects of promotion, identifying the starting base for brand association in sponsorship is challenging. One approach is to measure particular elements such as brand and event personality for the group exposed to the sponsorship, and to compare that to a control group that does not learn about the sponsorship. This experimental approach has shown that sponsorship can transfer image and further that this image transfer is enhanced when the brand and the event are matched at the start on either image or functionality (Gwinner & Eaton 1999).

Brand attitudes

Defined as overall evaluations of the brand in terms of its quality and the satisfaction it generates.

Measures of attitude toward sponsors as a result of their role as sponsor abound, as do attitudes toward the sponsor as an outcome of sponsoring. There is an important distinction between these two measures. In their role as sponsors, brands and corporations can be credited with supporting the event. This type of brand attitude measure typically captures feelings of reciprocity when the individual appreciates the support given to a charity, team, or arts festival. For example, the question might be if one agrees or disagrees with the statement: "FedEx's sponsorship of the golf tournament improves my impression of the company" (Irwin et al. 2003).

The second approach to attitude measurement seeks to capture changes in attitude toward the brand or company as a result of exposure to the sponsored event. This might reflect reciprocity or might be built from familiarity or exposure experiences. This second aspect of brand attitude typically stems from a post-event measure. Using the earlier example, respondents could be asked to agree/disagree with the statement: "I have a positive impression of FedEx." These are different measures and should not be thought of as interchangeable.

Sponsorship has at least three particular areas where attitude measurement is atypical as compared to other areas of promotion: concerns of commercialization, controversial partnerships, and property rivalries. The first challenging area in sponsoring is in terms of attitudes toward commercialization. For example, commercialization (acceptance or rejection of it) can influence college students' purchase of a sponsor's product (Zhang et al. 2005). Attitudes toward sponsors can be colored if there is also a sense of commercialization. This has been shown to be a sensitive topic in collegiate sports (McAllister 2010), stadium naming, and the arts (Finkel 2010). While there can be consumer support of sponsors, there can also be punishment of them if they seem to have a commercial preoccupation in their relationship to a team rather than a genuine interest.

Second, sponsorship must be sensitive to attitudes that come in reaction to the sponsorship by those against the alignment, such as in stadium naming (Chen & Zhang 2012). This may be related to commercialism but may also be a reaction to the sponsor or the resulting name. For instance, the name of Candlestick Park in San Francisco, California, changed to 3Com Park after a deal with 3Com Corporation and while people disliked this change, the next sponsorship deal was even less popular. The name "Monster Park" followed a deal with Monster Inc., a cable company. The local population preferred the original name, and voted in a referendum that the venue's name revert to Candlestick Park.

In Germany, researchers have found that it is not only feelings of commercialization that result in resistance to sponsors but perceptions of geographical or regional fit. Survey results from nearly 800 fans of German soccer team Borussia Dortmund found that regional identification of fans resulted in less receptivity to a new naming sponsorship relationship. The implication is that stadium renaming can be threatening to highly identified fans, who do not want their traditions and rituals to be changed (Woisetschläger et al. forthcoming).

Lastly, sport sponsorship comes with rivalries, which often means strong positive attitudes toward one's own team and strong negative attitudes against the main rival (Bergkvist 2012). When rivalries are very powerful, brands have even attempted to sponsor both arch-rivals, as for Glasgow clubs, Celtic and Rangers (Davies et al. 2006). Another approach to avoiding rivalry was trialed by Emirates Airlines when they sponsored referees from the

Professional Game Match Officials (Simon 2006) but they eventually dropped this relationship in favor of team and event sponsorships.

Over time, reactions to sponsorship have evolved as more and more people have experienced it and as it has become a common source of funding for grassroots local performing arts to large-scale municipal investments like stadiums. That said, ubiquity is not the same as acceptance. Cause sponsoring perhaps faces the most scrutiny when companies are suspected of utilizing the cause to compensate for a negative aspect of their business or business process. The sponsorship of environmental causes by oil companies, alcohol moderation awareness programs by beverage companies, and healthful sports by fast food companies are a few examples where consumer skepticism may arise and resulting attitudes may be difficult to assess.

Brand attachment

Defined as how loyal the customer feels toward the brand.

Brand loyalty is a special consideration as measured in sponsorship since many sponsorships seek to capitalize on existing property loyalty. While it can happen, it is not necessarily the case that team loyalty or arts patronage will translate into sponsor loyalty.

Researchers examining the potential of sponsorship to increase brand loyalty have found that one's own feeling of congruence with an event (in this case the 2008 Summer Olympics) and the fit between a brand (here, adidas and Samsung) and the event, both support loyalty (Mazodier & Merunka 2012). They argue that the change in reported brand loyalty from before to after an event could be described as coming from two processes. First, feelings of personal congruence with the event support brand loyalty through brand liking. Second, perceptions of fit between the brand and the event also support brand liking and brand trust and this in turn influences brand loyalty. So, when people feel they are part of the "event family," and when the sponsor and event "fit together well" this supports feelings that the person might "keep purchasing this brand" (Mazodier & Merunka 2012, p. 812).

Based on the work of Beatty & Kahle (1988), Jacoby & Chestnut (1978), and Dick & Basu (1994) on loyalty and commitment, Cornwell and Coote (2005) developed a measure of sponsorship-linked purchase commitment that captures how devoted a person is to purchase activities of sponsoring brands. The measure was utilized in a study of individuals participating in a Komen Foundation Race for the Cure event that supports breast cancer research. The four scale items used in the study were:

1. When choosing brands and retailers, I choose those that sponsor [the Race].
2. I would drive out of my way to buy from a sponsor of [the Race].
3. When a new sponsor joins [the Race], I switch my buying to support them.
4. I would choose to buy from a sponsor of [the Race], even if the prices of competitors were lower.

The study considered how individual participants identify with the event and those more strongly identified with the Race for the Cure showed more purchase commitment toward the sponsor's products.

Brand experience

Defined as the extent to which customers use the brand; talk to others about the brand; seek out brand information, promotions, and events.

Sponsorships that integrate the brand and the sponsored activity can be the essence of brand experience. For example, Starwood's youthful Aloft boutique hotel brand communicates via the sponsorship of music festivals (*Marketing Week* 2012). To promote its sponsorship of UK festivals "Hard Rock Calling" and "Wireless," Starwood offered preferred guests a chance to win a "Rockstar" experience at either event. Steven Taylor, Starwood's VP of marketing, explained that 90,000 people entered the competition and that they were able to track staying patterns to understand "who was staying with us more because of the contest" (p. 20). The incremental value of the sponsorship program was estimated to be $4 million over six months.

Sponsorship impact for business-to-business relationships

Because there are fewer business-to-business relationships than business-to-consumer relationships, the former can be easier to track. On the other hand, since business relationships may take longer to move from contact to contract, it can be difficult to track the influential factors. To measure relationship development and maintenance through sponsorship, interim measures of the outcomes of hospitality such as informal meetings and event participations might be useful.

In sponsorship and in other indirect marketing endeavors the idea of a purchase or action funnel is popular. Borrowing a page from early advertising research, awareness, interest, desire, and action are measured as a progression through a narrowing funnel of prospects toward the end goal of action (Lavidge & Steiner 1961). Many variants on this early model remain popular today. For example, some extend from the original four to include a fifth step, "advocacy." Others expand the original thinking to include industry-relevant steps such as trial or limited first-time purchase. Most funnels also examine the progression rate from one stage to the next as an additional piece of information. For instance, 60% of those becoming aware of the brand via sponsorship then expressed interest by subsequently visiting the website of the company.

To measure sponsorship outcomes in business-to-business relationships a company may view a number of behaviors as movements along a process that ends in buying. Researchers will use the term "variable" or "construct" for these steps in a process and may link them together in a model. These types of variables may be part of a causal chain, meaning that one step influences the next. For example, one might want to examine a chain of events whereby exposure to a sponsor's message via attending a hospitality event leads to product evaluation and preference formation, and in turn purchase. As in consumer relationships, sales are of interest, but in business-to-business relationships, increased account profitability and number of referrals for new business may be other outcomes to be measured (Collett 2008). Importantly, the role sponsorship plays in this process should be specifically outlined if sponsorship is to be held accountable.

Sponsorship impact on marketing assets

In addition to measuring sponsorship influence on individual customer, viewer, and attendee mindsets, one can also measure impacts on marketing assets in both business-to-consumer and business-to-business sponsoring. Measuring perceptions of variables such as brand equity or perceptions of loyalty is not the same as measuring financial brand equity or profitability due to loyal consumers. Still, as an interim measure or as a benchmarking tool, perceptual data can be very informative.

Marketing assets "are customer-focused measures of the value of the firm (and its offerings) that may enhance the firm's long-term value" (Rust et al. 2004, p.78) and the two most researched are brand equity and customer equity. Determining brand equity and customer equity can be a lengthy process but it is also possible simply to ask questions of fans, attendees, and consumers of a sponsor's product or service and obtain perceptual measures.

As an example, one summary measure of brand equity that was developed with international measurement in mind (Yoo & Donthu 2001) has the following four items:

1. It makes sense to buy brand X instead of any other brand, even if they are the same.

2. Even if another brand has the same features as brand X, I would prefer to buy brand X.
3. If there is another brand as good as brand X, I prefer to buy brand X.
4. If another brand is not different from brand X in any way, it seems smarter to purchase brand X.

This scale of brand equity has been utilized in measuring the way in which sport team sponsorship contributes to sponsor brand equity (Wang et al. 2011).

As a growing area of marketing and advertising research, sponsorship measurement has imported a number of measurement instruments, primarily scales from these parent disciplines. Some measures have been adapted to the sponsorship context and some have been developed specifically for it. One controversial area of measurement deserves further discussion and this is the concept of congruence.

Measurement of congruence

Congruence, also called match or fit, is a central idea in sponsoring and has historically been shown to be beneficial. For instance, the congruence in people's minds about a running event being sponsored by a company that makes running shoes is believed to support acceptance, memory, and even attitudes. The concept of congruence in sponsorship has been borrowed from marketing where it was originally taken from the study of personality in psychology. Congruence has been thought of as functional or image similarity (Gwinner 1997), as native or created fit (Becker-Olsen & Simmons 2002), and as self-evident or strategic linking (Cornwell 1995). While these differences are useful characterizations, are they tapping into the real source of congruence?

One of the earliest and, to date, most popular measures of fit is a short five-item scale that was used to measure response to possible sponsor and event combinations (Speed & Thompson 2000).

1. There is a logical connection between the event and the sponsor.
2. The image of the event and the image of the sponsor are similar.
3. The sponsor and the event fit together well.
4. The company and the event stand for similar things.
5. It makes sense to me that this company sponsors this event.

The research showed that fit between sponsor and property interacts with other variables in determining sponsorship response. For example, when individuals have personal liking for the event, a sponsor that fits well with the event will respond even more positively to the event (Speed & Thompson 2000).

In the sponsorship of social causes, fit has been measured with semantic differentials such as the following set of seven items (Simmons & Becker-Olsen 2006):

1. dissimilar/similar;
2. inconsistent/consistent;
3. atypical/typical;
4. unrepresentative/representative;
5. not complementary/complementary;
6. low fit/high fit; and
7. does not make sense/makes sense.

This measure of fit was utilized in research examining fit between a social cause, for example, the Special Olympics and either a brand of dog food, Alpo, or a retail brand, Sports Authority. The findings showed that poor fit between sponsor and property could be overcome by engaging in activities that create fit such as connecting pets and pet care to children and happy childhoods via explanation and giveaways.

While these early measures of fit were successful and useful in the contexts where employed, sponsorship has been evolving and gaining acceptance, changing the ways in which people think about it. For example, in the 1990s sponsorship was not as widespread a communications platform as it is today. Individuals may not have understood why an insurance company would want to sponsor a ballet troupe. Over time, people have come to understand and even expect sponsorship as a part of events, games, festivals, and competitions. Thus, when a respondent encounters questions about the sponsorship relationship "making sense," they may not be responding to the particular pairing but to the ubiquity of sponsoring.

Researchers from Australia reviewed available definitions of congruence and decided that a measure built around two dimensions: relevance (when a particular sponsor–sponsee relationship makes sense and has meaning), and expectancy (when a sponsor–sponsee relationship could be expected) would be useful (Fleck & Quester 2007). There was already thinking that congruence had two components (Heckler & Childers 1992) but measures had to be developed. Through a process of scale development, beginning with as many items as candidates for the new scale, the authors reduced their evaluation to a set of six items:

Expectancy

- E1: I am not surprised that this company sponsors this event.
- E2: One would expect this company to sponsor this event.
- E3: It was predictable that this company would sponsor this event.

Relevancy

- R1: That this company sponsors this event tells me something about it.
- R2: When I hear of this sponsorship, I can understand (Company/Brand X) better.
- R3: With this sponsorship, I discover a new aspect of this company.

Their further work suggested reducing the relevancy items to only two, one focused on meaning and the other on newness (R1 and R3), but in many applications the two items oriented to understanding the firm (R1 and R2) may be more valuable. These researchers subsequently tested their scale in France and Australia and found it useful. It has the ability to capture congruence in a different way. The authors argue that this measure can help managers gauge the freshness of their sponsorship program. Importantly, these more precise measures focus on the particular relationship that a respondent should be evaluating.

Still, there are issues with the measurement of congruence or fit and with the central role that it plays in sponsorship evaluation. The concern is that managers utilizing an established fit measure may have a false sense of the effectiveness of their communications via sponsorship. This may be especially problematic when the relationship might invoke skepticism or criticism. Researchers have shown that individuals attribute at least four types of motives to corporate social responsibility programs: values-driven motives, stakeholder and strategic ones, and ego motives (Ellen et al. 2006). Consumers will accept "values-driven" motives such as benevolence, and may accept "stakeholder-driven" motives where responsibility programs are expected and even "strategic-driven" motives where work with the social cause aligns with business goals. The last group, however, "egoistic-driven" motives, are those that exploit rather than nurture the cause. Thus, when the cause is used to counter a firm's image issues this is less acceptable.

For instance, consider the sponsorship relationship between Shell Oil Company and Ducks Unlimited, a wetlands conservation group. In fit measurement, this relationship may "make sense" or "be expected" but possibly because the perceiver knows that the firm is concerned with their reputation relative to the environment. Importantly, while the company and non-profit may have things in common, such as an orientation to the natural environment, the relationship may invoke skepticism. Even if Shell Oil has a valid reputation claim of helping preserve wetlands, unless one is knowledgeable about the particular case, it may be difficult to discern when a brand is only seeking to communicate an environmentally friendly image. Consumers may attribute to them an egoistic, image-enhancing motive. A fit measure may, however, return a finding of "high fit" that means that people understand why the company is a sponsor but they may or may not be comfortable with the relationship (Pappu & Cornwell 2012).

In short, if the motives of a sponsorship could be questioned with regard to image, "Are you engaging in this sponsorship to look more healthy or environmentally friendly" or ulterior agendas, then similarity may fuel skepticism and negatively impact brand values. Thus, while a pharmaceutical company may be questioned if supporting a cancer research cause, their goodwill might be readily approved if supporting homeless shelters. Brands should fully understand the nature of their congruence with a property. Particularly if there is the possibility of an egoistic or ulterior motive interpretation on the part of important audiences, sponsors should begin by measuring areas of similarity and fit alongside other factors before engaging in a sponsorship.

References

Ambler, T., Bhattacharya, C. B., Edell, J., Keller, K. L., Lemon, K. N. & Mittal, V. (2002). Relating Brand and Customer Perspectives on Marketing Management. *Journal of Services Research, 5,* 1, 13–25.

Association of National Advertisers and International Events Group (2010). 2010 ANA/IEG Survey Research Report Sponsorship and Events Measurement, 1–43. Retrieved November 27, 2013 from http://www.sponsorship.c.om/IEG/files/d9/d97183e0-ae38-4aa7-a137-75fb930a7483.pdf.

Beatty, S. E. & Kahle, L. R. (1988). Alternative Hierarchies of the Attitude–Behavior Relationship: The Impact of Brand Commitment and Habit. *Journal of the Academy of Marketing Science, 16,* 3, 1–10.

Becker-Olsen, K. & Simmons, C. J. (2002). When Do Social Sponsorships Enhance or Dilute Equity? Fit, Message Source and the Persistence of Effects. *Advances in Consumer Research, 29,* 287–89.

Bergkvist, L. (2012). The Flipside of the Sponsorship Coin: Do You Still Buy the Beer When the Brewer Underwrites a Rival Team? *Journal of Advertising Research,* March, 65–73.

Chen, K. K. & Zhang, J. J. (2012). To Name It or Not Name It: Consumer Perspectives on Facility Naming Rights Sponsorship in Collegiate Athletics. *Journal of Issues in Intercollegiate Athletics, 2,* 119–48.

Collett, P. (2008). Sponsorship-related Hospitality: Planning for Measureable Success. *Journal of Sponsorship, 1,* 3, 286–96.

Cornwell, T. B. (1995). Sponsorship-linked Marketing Development. *Sport Marketing Quarterly, 4,* 4, 13–24.

Cornwell, T. B. (2008). State of the Art and Science in Sponsorship-linked Marketing. *Journal of Advertising, 37*, 3, 41–55.

Cornwell, T. B. & Coote, L. V. (2005). Corporate Sponsorship of a Cause: The Role of Identification in Purchase Intent. *Journal of Business Research, 58*, 3, 268–76.

Cornwell, T. B., Weeks, C. S. & Roy, D. P. (2005). Sponsorship-linked Marketing: Opening the Black Box. *Journal of Advertising, 34*, 2, 23–45.

Cornwell, T. B., Humphreys, M. S., Maguire, A. M., Weeks, C. S. & Tellegen, C. L. (2006). Sponsorship-linked Marketing: The Role of Articulation in Memory. *Journal of Consumer Research, 33*, 3, 312–21.

Crompton, J. L. (2004). Conceptualization and Alternate Operationalizations of the Measurement of Sponsorship Effectiveness in Sport. *Leisure Studies, 23*, 3, 267–81.

Davies, F., Veloutsou, C. & Costa, A. (2006). Investigating the Influence of a Joint Sponsorship of Rival Teams on Supporter Attitudes and Brand Preferences. *Journal of Marketing Communications, 12*, 1, 31–48.

Dick, A. S. & Basu, K. (1994). Customer Loyalty: Toward an Integrated Conceptual Framework. *Journal of the Academy of Marketing Science, 22*, 2, 99–113.

Ellen, P. S., Webb, D. J. & Mohr, L. A. (2006). Building Corporate Associations: Consumer Attributions for Corporate Social Responsibility Programs. *Journal of the Academy of Marketing Science, 34*, 2, 147–57.

Finkel, R. (2010). Re-imaging Arts Festivals through a Corporate Lens: A Case Study of Business Sponsorship at the Henley Festival. *Managing Leisure, 15*, 237–50.

Fleck, N. D. & Quester, P. (2007). Birds of a Feather Flock Together . . . Definition, Role and Measure of Congruence: An Application to Sponsorship. *Psychology & Marketing, 24*, 11, 975–1000.

Grohs, R., Wagner, U. & Vsetecka, S. (2004). Assessing the Effectiveness of Sport Sponsorships—An Empirical Investigation. *Schmalenbach Business Review, 56*, 2, 119–38.

Gwinner, K. (1997). A Model of Image Creation and Image Transfer in Event Sponsorship. *International Marketing Review, 14*, 145–58.

Gwinner, K. & Eaton, J. (1999). Building Brand Image through Event Sponsorship: The Role of Image Transfer. *Journal of Advertising, 28*, 4, 47–57.

Hammer, M. (2007). The 7 Deadly Sins of Performance Measurement and How to Avoid Them. *MIT Sloan Management Review, 48*, 3, 19–28.

Heckler, S. E. & Childers, T. L. (1992). The Role of Expectancy and Relevancy in Memory for Verbal and Visual Information: What Is Incongruency? *Journal of Consumer Research, 18*, 475–92.

Irwin, R. L., Lachowetz, T., Cornwell, T. B. & Clark, J. S. (2003). Cause-related Sport Sponsorship: An Assessment of Spectator Beliefs, Attitudes and Behavioral Intentions. *Sport Marketing Quarterly, 12*, 2, 131–39.

Jacoby, J. & Chestnut, R. W. (1978). *Brand Loyalty: Measurement and Management.* New York: Wiley.

Johar, G. V. & Pham, M. T. (1999). Relatedness, Prominence, and Constructive Sponsor Identification. *Journal of Marketing Research, 36*, 3, 299–312.

Johar, G. V., Pham, M. T. & Wakefield, K. L. (2006). How Event Sponsors Are Really Identified: A (Baseball) Field Analysis. *Journal of Advertising Research*, 46, 2, 183–98.

Joyce Julius & Associates (2013). *About Us*. Retrieved October 5, 2013 from http://www.joycejulius.com/index.html.

Karp, A. (2013). Jimmie Johnson Topped All NASCAR Drivers in Sponsor Exposure During Fox' Races. *Sports Business Daily*, June 20. Retrieved October 5, 2013 from http://m.sportsbusinessdaily.com/Daily/Issues/2013/06/20/Research-and-Ratings/NASCAR.aspx.

Keller, K. L. (1993). Conceptualizing, Measuring, and Managing Customer-based Brand Equity. *Journal of Marketing*, 57, 1, 1–22.

Lavidge, R. & Steiner, G. A. (1961). A Model for Predictive Measurements of Advertising Effectiveness. *Journal of Marketing*, 25, October, 59–62.

Marketing Week (2012). Brand and Bands Make Music Festival Experience. *Marketing Week*, 35, 6, 20.

Mazodier, M. & Merunka, D. (2012). Achieving Brand Loyalty through Sponsorship: The Role of Fit and Self-congruity. *Journal of the Academy of Marketing Science*, 40, 6, 807–20.

McAllister, M. P. (2010). Hypercommercialism, Televisuality, and the Changing Nature of College Sports Sponsorship. *American Behavioral Scientist*, 53, 10, 1476–91.

Meenaghan, T. (2011). Mind the Gap in Sponsorship Measurement. *ADMAP*, February, 34–6.

Oakes, S. (2003). Demographic and Sponsorship Considerations for Jazz and Classical Music Festivals. *The Service Industries Journal*, 23, 3, 165–78.

Pappu, R. & Cornwell, T. B. (2012). The Role of Fit and Similarity in Social Sponsorship Communication. *AMA Summer Educators' Conference Proceedings*, 23, 103–04.

Rust, R. T., Ambler, T., Carpenter, G. S., Kumar, V. & Srivastava, R. K. (2004). Measuring Marketing Productivity: Current Knowledge and Future Directions. *Journal of Marketing*, 28, 4, 76–89.

Simmons, C. J. & Becker-Olsen, K. L. (2006). Achieving Marketing Objectives through Social Sponsorships. *Journal of Marketing*, 70, 4, 154–69.

Simon, M. (2006). Emirates to Drop Ref Sponsorship. *Marketing*, August 9, 2.

Speed, R. & Thompson, P. (2000). Determinants of Sports Sponsorship Response. *Journal of the Academy of Marketing Science*, 28, 226–38.

Tripodi, J. A., Hirons, M., Bednall, D. & Sutherland, M. (2003). Cognitive Evaluation: Prompts Used to Measure Sponsorship Awareness. *International Journal of Market Research*, 45, 4, 435–55.

Wang, M. C-H., Cheng, J. M-S., Purwanto, B. M. & Erimurti, K. (2011). The Determinants of the Sports Team Sponsor's Brand Equity: A Cross-Country Comparison in Asia. *International Journal of Market Research*, 53, 6, 811–29.

Whitney, T. (2013). Can Sponsorship Impact Brand Affinity? Retrieved October 6, 2013 from http://www.business2community.com/branding/can-sponsorship-impact-brand-affinity-0630244.

Woisetschläger, D. M., Haselhoff, V. & Backhaus, C. (forthcoming). Fans' Resistance to Naming Right Sponsorships—Why Stadium Names Remain the Same for Fans. *The European Journal of Marketing*.

Yoo, B. & Donthu, N. (2001) Developing and Validating a Multidimensional Consumer-based Brand Equity Scale. *Journal of Business Research*, *52*, 1, 1–14.

Zhang, Z., Won, D. & Pastore, D.L. (2005). The Effects of Attitudes toward Commercialization on College Students' Purchasing Intentions of Sponsors' Products. *Sport Marketing Quarterly*, *14*, 3, 177–87.

8

EVALUATING SPONSORSHIPS

Sponsorship evaluation can be thought of as a systematic gathering and assessment of information to provide useful feedback about sponsorships to support decision-making. Sponsorship evaluation depends heavily on sponsorship measurement, but includes more than measurement of any individual, or even portfolio of sponsorships. Measurement of sponsorship should ideally feed back into a comprehensive evaluation system. Over the past two decades there has been a shift toward measurement of return on marketing investments (Seggie et al. 2007), an emphasis which is overdue in sponsorship.

It is worthwhile to note that the term "evaluation" is utilized here rather than terms such as "measurement of effectiveness" or "marketing measurement." The reason is to draw a clear line between the assessment of outcomes coming from sponsorship in terms of recall, attitude, or purchase behavior and the evaluation of overall performance of the program. Just as goals and touchdowns or wins and losses do not provide the complete picture of a successful sporting season, so too measurement of sponsorship outcomes is not the full picture of a successful partnership.

Return on investment

Much of the discussion in sponsorship evaluation centers on Return on Investment (ROI). This simple measure is calculated by taking the gains of an investment minus the cost of the investment, divided by the cost of the investment. ROI is anything but simple to utilize when evaluating the loose connections between sponsorship and purchase of the sponsors' products.

The main challenge in calculating ROI for sponsorship is much like that of advertising—isolating the effects of sponsorship from everything else.

Perhaps it is most clear to see the challenge through an example of when effects could possibly be isolated. If we have a brand new product that a market has never seen before and it is promoted through a sponsorship relationship where the only way to purchase the product is to follow a communicated link to an online ordering system, we could be fairly certain that the sponsorship delivered those online sales. In this situation, with a new, never-marketed product, we have no carry over effects from previous marketing communications and no past brand experience on the part of consumers. With communication about the product provided only at the sponsored event we have no confusion with other contemporaneous messages. This is a rare event.

To begin to isolate the return on marketing investment from sponsorship in complex, long-standing programs, a baseline is needed, as is some measure of other contributors to marketing success (or failure). Calculating return on a sponsorship investment allows investments to be compared and evaluated against other outlays, but what is really needed is a more comprehensive evaluation system. A method that better evaluates the values stemming from marketing expenditures is also one that supports accountability.

Evaluation and accountability

It has been argued for some time that the failure of marketing to be accountable in terms of adding value to an organization has threatened marketing's existence as a distinct capability (Rust et al. 2004a). In particular, there is pressure for marketing activities of all kinds to be more financially accountable. In sponsorship, there has been considerable effort to develop such yardsticks, but these measures are data that go into an evaluation and are only an interim step toward financial accountability.

David Stewart, Professor of Marketing at University of California, Riverside, is another scholar urging greater accountability in marketing (Stewart 2009). Several points basic to marketing are useful in framing the discussion for sponsorship. First, the argument that marketing is highly idiosyncratic and thus difficult to evaluate in any standardized way is criticized by analogy to the quality movement. Stewart notes:

> And just as we hear today that identifying standard processes that work across many industries is difficult, so it was at the beginning of the quality movement when critics suggested that applying the same metrics and processes to industries as different as jet engines, pharmaceuticals, hotel chains, and consumer packaged goods was impossible.
>
> *Stewart (2009, p. 638)*

He argues that the importance of establishing standards is a lesson marketers can learn from the quality movement. In turn, it is a lesson sponsorship can learn from marketing.

Stewart goes on to describe three types of return on marketing: short-term incremental effects, long-term persistent effects, and real options that may be pursued in the future. Short-term measures are familiar: incremental sales, awareness, brand preference, and purchase intention, all of which are also common in sponsorship. Long-term measures such as brand equity, market share, and customer loyalty can be measured too. Short-term and long-term measures are candidates for standardization but real options are, by their very nature, unique. Real options, originating in financial discussions, are opportunities that may be pursued in the future and sponsorship abounds in them: image building that supports future actions' relationships with options to renew into the future; brand development with unique associations that drive brand value and distinctiveness and connectivity across industries. Importantly, outcomes in these three areas must be linked to financial performance.

The last requirement to make sponsorship accountable is a formal process to link actions to intermediate outcomes and then to financial results. It should be noted that this discussion could be applied even to non-profits where the ultimate result may be donations, volunteer hours, or cause support. The key is to identify important drivers of the end goal of interest, then identify intermediate measures linked to these results. For example, hospitality hours at an event may be related to customer acquisition, which in turn may lead to new business. Stewart argues, "Once the identification of all these linkages is complete, they can be put together into a causal model with a marketing activity giving rise to specific outcomes that are measurable with specific metrics" (2009). If a sponsorship action does not have an identifiable outcome, it is likely to be called into question.

Evaluative models and systems

Many evaluation models in marketing have adopted brand equity as their focus (Shankar et al. 2008). For example, one marketing/branding company, Interbrand, combines financial, demand, and competitive analysis to determine brand value, which is measured as net present value of brand earnings (Interbrand 2013). Another brand equity model is Corebrand. In determining the percentage of market capitalization that is derived from the corporate brand, Corebrand utilizes survey responses regarding familiarity and favorability. These measures are combined with others to calculate the value of the brand (Corebrand 2013).

A Multicategory Brand Equity model for Allstate Insurance was developed to capture, in part, advertising as an investment (Shankar et al. 2008) and serves as an example in which sponsorship expenditures are considered in modeling. Allstate has for many years held an extensive sponsorship portfolio, including football and soccer as well as a focus on the Olympic Games. Researchers compiled financial data, including cash flow by product category (e.g., auto insurance, life insurance), and customer data including brand perceptions, choice, and brand image. In addition, marketing communication expenditures were incorporated. The results of the model showed that marketing communications had a strong, positive long-term influence on brand equity and shareholder value.

Applying a managerial perspective, the Balanced Scorecard method was developed as a way to capture the value of both tangible and intangible assets to the firm (Kaplan & Norton 1992). This multifaceted evaluation tool considers customer, internal learning, business process, and financial information. This approach has been criticized because it "does not allow for any causal interpretations to be made as to the direct impact of marketing actions on the long-term financial performance of the firm" (Seggie et al. 2007, p. 839). Still, this approach is widely utilized to gain a bird's-eye view of firm assets and to integrate its disparate parts.

A comprehensive marketing model, Customer Lifetime Value (CLV), combines customer value equity (what the customer believes the utility of the brand to be), brand equity (the customer's assessment of the brand over and above the perceived value), and retention equity (loyalty of the customer to the brand) (Rust et al. 2000, 2004b). In evaluation, this model focuses on customers over their lifetime with the company rather than the brand, but it does link marketing action to financial returns.

One application of the Customer Lifetime Value approach in sponsorship utilized a multi-wave survey design (Nickell 2010). In examining the financial value of sponsorship for a restaurant chain sponsoring a college football bowl game, six phases of data collection were used. The focus was to determine purchasing behavior and brand attitudes of attendees before and after the sponsored event, and these data were examined in comparison to television viewers of the event and to the general public. Findings showed that the model accurately predicted the number of new customers for the sponsor's products after one buying cycle. The model was also able to establish the financial return on the sponsorship investment by estimating the customer lifetime value (CLV) of these new buyers.

Context-dependent assessment

Researchers from Finland (Frösén et al. 2013) have provided evidence that marketing performance assessment systems are contextual in nature. That is, the most effective system is likely the system that best fits the firm and its environment. Based on a survey of over 1,000 Finnish managers, these researchers identified nine dimensions of marketing performance: brand equity, market position, financial position, long-term firm value, innovation, customer feedback, customer equity, channel activity (distribution manage- ment), and sales process. The combination of these metrics varies across companies in different industries and at different stages. This is easily applied to sponsoring. For fast-moving consumer goods (FMCG) firms investing heavily in sponsoring, their profiles should reflect emphasis on measuring brand equity where customer attitudes, perceptions, thoughts, and feelings are captured. For business-to-business firms investing in sponsorship, the emphasis may be on customer equity, channel activity, and sales processes.

Non-financial evaluation

While many evaluation discussions focus on Return on Investment (ROI), an additional or in some cases alternative measure, Return on Objectives (ROO) can also be useful for sponsorship. The primary reason to utilize ROO is that the metric for the organization is non-financial. The vast majority of sponsors are for-profit organizations, yet, non-profits make up a huge portion of those sponsored. Indeed, non-profits, government institutions, ministries, and non-governmental organizations (NGOs) all engage in sponsorship.

An excellent example is the sponsorship of NASCAR by the US Army. The main sponsorship goal of the US Army, as well as that of the National Guard, US Air Force, Navy, and Marine Corps, is recruitment. The objective of these organizations is to increase the number of recruits though building exposure, interest, and image for the armed forces. While there may not be financially measurable "gains" from the investment, there can, nonetheless, be financial accountability of the sponsorships employed relative to other marketing approaches through analysis of ROO.

It is also the case that in evaluating the influence of a marketing communi- cations activity on behavior such as volunteering, recruiting, or behavior avoidance (e.g., quitting smoking), it is difficult to isolate influence. John Myers of the Army Marketing and Research Group explains, "You can't really attribute one visit to a NASCAR race by a prospect-age youth as resulting in actually raising his or her right arm and swearing on the oath . . . It is a conversation that may start at the NASCAR track. It may start somewhere else and continue at the track" (Long 2012). Groups may find it hard to put a financial value on behaviors and changes in attitude or they may find it objectionable, so the use of return on objectives becomes more viable.

A third sponsorship evaluation metric, Return on Relationships (ROR), is "the long-term net financial outcome caused by the establishment and maintenance of an organization's network of relationships" (Gummesson

2004). While the idea of measuring a return on relationships has gained currency in social media, the original thinking, based on industrial relationships, has not been developed in sponsorship. The approach examines investments in relationships and evaluates joint productivity gains and incremental values (Grönroos & Helle 2012).

The applicability of return on relationships to sponsorship is clear considering that a sponsor can do as much to improve the image of an event as an event does to support the image of a sponsor (Walker et al. 2011). An interesting example of developing unique relationships comes from luxury watch manufacturer, Hublot. As sponsors of the UEFA EURO 2008 tournament, they devoted their entire billboard allocation to "Unite Against Racism," a pan-European campaign against racism in soccer. The expensive communications space drew a great deal of commentary. Hublot was credited both for being genuine in their relationship and for gaining extensive positive media coverage for the brand (McDermott 2009).

The starting points and the accountability mindset

If a system of evaluation is not in place then how best to begin? One starting point is to take stock of all measures currently undertaken in the organization that would be useful for evaluation. Green (2008) suggests an audit of four types of data: financial (e.g., sales, profits, market share), behavioral (e.g., brand purchase, loyalty), perceptual (e.g., brand awareness, attitudes), and exposure (e.g., target reach and frequency of exposure). In this stocktaking it is important not to keep a measure just because it is available. Conversely, any needed measures should be identified. As Stewart notes, intermediate measures should be linked to financial results. As a start, it may be useful to examine correlations between intermediate measures and financial returns, but the end goal should be to identify causal linkages.

The accountability of marketing in financial terms has enjoyed two decades of discussion leading to various evaluation models and systems. This conversation is now taking place in the realm of sponsorship. But how does one begin to develop an accountability mindset? One perspective is that it can begin among those being trained to go into the industry. The idea is that early training utilizing spreadsheets to inculcate marketing accountability may improve the situation (Ganesh & Paswan 2010). It is difficult to say how many individuals employed in the sponsorship industry, property side and brand side, have extensive analytical experience. It does seem, however, that more fluidity with analytics supports not only practical analysis but also conceptual skills.

Importantly, while oriented to selling, the brand side thinking on evaluation is more informed by marketing science, whereas the property side may be more oriented towards financing, such as selling tickets in sports, or increasing philanthropy in the arts. The selling orientation in sport properties begins with ticket sales but extends to sponsorships where staff are incentivized to sell, with rewards such as tickets to an event (Farrelly & Greyser 2012). In the arts, the long-standing orientations to philanthropy, to social influence, and to community image (O'Hagan & Harvey 2000) do not promote forthright discussions of return on investment—although likely it is relevant. While there may be initial disagreement on what appropriate evaluation should be, having upfront discussions over what should be measured and how measures will feed into an evaluation system will only support the sponsorship relationship.

References

Corebrand (2013). Correlating Brand with Financial Performance. Retrieved October 4, 2013 from http://www.corebrand.com/brandpower/methodology.

Farrelly, F. & Greyser, S. (2012). Sponsorship Linked Internal Marketing (SLIM): A Strategic Platform for Employee Engagement and Business Performance. *Journal of Sport Management, 26*, 506–20.

Frösén, J., Tikkanen, H., Jaakkola, M. & Vassinen, A. (2013). Marketing Performance Assessment Systems and the Business Context. *European Journal of Marketing, 47*, 5/6, 715–37.

Ganesh, G. & Paswan, A. K. (2010). Teaching Basic Marketing Accountability Using Spreadsheets: An Exploratory Perspective. *Journal of Business Research, 63*, 182–90.

Green, A. (2008). Planning for Effective Evaluation: Are Marketers Really Doing It? *Journal of Sponsorship, 1*, 4, 357–63.

Grönroos, C. & Helle, P. (2012). Return on Relationships: Conceptual Understanding and Measurement of Mutual Gains from Relational Business Engagements. *Journal of Business & Industrial Marketing, 27*, 5, 344–59.

Gummesson, E. (2004). Return on Relationships (ROR): The Value of Relationship Marketing and CRM in Business-to-Business Contexts. *Journal of Business & Industrial Marketing, 19*, 2, 136–48.

Interbrand (2013). Best Global Brands Our Methodology. Retrieved October 4, 2013 from http://www.interbrand.com/en/best-global-brands/2013/best-global-brands-methodology.aspx.

Kaplan, R. S. & Norton, D. P. (1992). The Balanced Scorecard—Measures That Drive Performance. *Harvard Business Review, 70*, 1, 71–9.

Long, D. (2012). U.S. Army to Discontinue NASCAR Sponsorship in 2013. *USA Today*, July 10. Retrieved October 8, 2013 from http://usatoday30.usatoday.com/sports/motor/nascar/story/2012-07-10/Army-wont-return-to-NASCAR-in-2013/56126666/1.

McDermott, M. (2009). Hublot & the Future of Watches—Jean Claude Biver Interview Baselworld 2009. Retrieved November 25, 2013 from http://www.ablogtowatch.com/hublot-the-future-of-watches-jean-claude-biver-interview-baselworld-2009/.

Nickell, D. (2010). The Drivers of a Successful Corporate Sponsorship and the Quantified Financial Impact: Applying the Attitudinal Triad of Cognition, Affect, and Conation and Customer Lifetime Value to Corporate Sponsorships (Doctoral Dissertation). Retrieved November 20, 2013 from *Marketing Dissertations*, Paper 17, http://scholarworks.gsu.edu/marketing_diss/17.

O'Hagan, J. & Harvey, D. (2000). Why Do Companies Sponsor Arts Events? Some Evidence and a Proposed Classification. *Journal of Cultural Economics*, *24*, 205–24.

Rust, R. T., Zeithaml, V. A. & Lemon, K. N. (2000). *Driving Customer Equity: How Customer Lifetime Value is Reshaping Corporate Strategy*. New York: The Free Press.

Rust, R. T., Ambler, T., Carpenter, G. S., Kumar, V. & Sirvastava, R. K. (2004a). Measuring Marketing Productivity: Current Knowledge and Future Directions. *Journal of Marketing*, *69*, October, 76–89.

Rust, R. T., Lemon, K. N. & Zeithaml, V. A. (2004b). Return on Marketing: Using Customer Equity to Focus Marketing Strategy. *Journal of Marketing*, *68*, 1, 109–27.

Seggie, S. H., Cavusgil, E. & Phelan, S. E. (2007). Measurement of Return on Marketing Investment: A Conceptual Framework and the Future of Marketing Metrics. *Industrial Marketing Management*, *36*, 834–41.

Shankar, V., Azar, P. & Fuller, M. (2008). BRAN*EQT: A Multicategory Brand Equity Model and Its Application at Allstate. *Marketing Science*, *27*, 4, 567–84.

Stewart, D. W. (2009). Marketing Accountability: Linking Marketing Actions to Financial Results. *Journal of Business Research*, *62*, 636–43.

Walker, M., Hall, T., Todd, S. Y. & Kent, A. (2011). Does Your Sponsor Affect My Perception of the Event? The Role of Event Sponsors as a Signal. *Sport Marketing Quarterly*, *20*, 138–47.

9
AMBUSHING AND LEGAL ISSUES IN SPONSORSHIP

Many will remember the UEFA European Championship soccer games, held in June 2012, thanks to some "lucky pants." Arsenal striker, Nicklas Bendtner, after scoring for Denmark against Portugal, raised his shirt in celebration, *and* in display of his Paddy Power underwear. Paddy Power, an Irish online betting company, is known for their cheeky promotional style and was immediately suspected for being behind Bendtner's choice of undergarment.

While Bendtner claimed he was just wearing a pair of lucky boxer shorts and didn't know that he was breaking the rules, he still received a fine of 100,000 euros and a one-game ban for his behavior. Telling, is the fact that Paddy Power paid Bendtner's fine. In understanding the size of the fine and the ambushing implications, it is important to know that the Denmark team had an exclusive sponsorship agreement with rival betting firm Ladbrokes (Sharma 2012). This exemplifies the essence of ambushing—a true sponsor (having paid for the rights of association with a property) loses the limelight to a direct competitor through that competitor's event-related activity. The fact that it was also a breach of UEFA's rule against communicating personal messages seems less important.

The stakes are high when brands pay millions to have an exclusive relationship with a property. For example, US automaker Chevrolet paid $559 million for a seven-year relationship with the British football (soccer) team Manchester United that runs through the 2020–21 season. Putting this in perspective, $691 million pays for automotive investments in Mexico including a $211 million expansion of the General Motors Toluca plant as well as $349 million for a new transmissions plant in Silao, and $131 million to expand to a next generation transmission plant in San Luis Potosi (*Business*

Insider 2013). While the Manchester United deal at $80 million per year is heralded as the most expensive shirt sponsorship in European soccer, other amounts to Barcelona ($38 million per year from Qatar Airways) and Bayern Munich ($37 million per year from Deutsche Telekom) (Colao 2013) also make it clear why true sponsors are sensitive to ambushing.

What is ambushing?

Perhaps no other area tied to sponsoring creates as much controversy and excitement as ambushing. Ideas about what ambushing is are still evolving and new definitions are being introduced, frequently in an effort to match current behaviors in the marketplace. The overwhelming majority of publicized ambushing centers on large sport events but it is also becoming commonplace in small, even grassroots events. Legal issues around ambushing take center stage because those seeking legal recourse must refer to a fabric of many laws never envisioned to address sponsorship activities rather than one single piece of directly relevant legislation.

Most important to sponsorship are intellectual property rights. Trademarks, copyrights, patents, trade secrets, and publicity rights, along with other laws depending on the jurisdiction, make a bundle of legal rights held by an owner. These may be used by the owner of the rights or licensed to specific others for use, and importantly, prohibited for use by particular others. Still, there are limits on the rights holder and any licensors, which seek to balance these specific rights with benefits that should come to others in society. In sum:

> intellectual property laws, thus, attempt to grant just enough rights to use and exclude others from using property to maximize the creation of intellectual property consistent with not unduly restricting other beneficial societal activities, importantly including freedom of speech and the press, economic competition and creative intellectual activities that build upon prior efforts of others to provide something new for society.
>
> *Phelps (2013)*

Intellectual property rights are the centerpiece of law for sponsorship, but various laws also exist to protect against misleading marketing practices (e.g., European Directive 2006/114/EC concerning misleading and comparative advertising) and unfair and deceptive advertising (e.g., laws under US, Federal Trade Commission Division of Advertising Practices). State, provincial, and local laws may also apply to aspects of sponsoring and in particular ambushing. The challenge begins with defining sponsorship and ambushing relative to current law.

One of the earliest definitions found ambush marketing to be the formation of an association with an event without securing official sponsorship rights (Sandler & Shani 1989). There was, initially, an emphasis on the ambusher's intent to be mistaken as a true sponsor and thereby usurp the position and the accruing benefits of being sponsor. This thinking has evolved over time and it is now recognized that "being thought of as an official sponsor" is not the goal for all those seeking a relationship with an event. This thinking also placed an emphasis on the official sponsor's rights and suggested that activities labeled "ambushing" might be illegal or unethical.

Nearly a decade later, Townley et al. (1998) also took a legal emphasis in their definition. Their wording, based in a sport context, describes ambush marketing as:

> unauthorized association by businesses of their names, brands, products or services with a sports event or competition through any one of a wide range of marketing activities; unauthorized in the sense that the controller of the commercial rights in such events, usually the relevant governing body, has neither sanctioned nor licensed the association, either itself or through commercial agents.
>
> *Townley et al. (1998, p. 1)*

Discussions about ambush marketing have evolved in the last decade to the point where one is reduced at times to describing what is undertaken as a way of better understanding the phenomenon. "Ambushing activities include use of phrases and images associated with the event or activity, purchase of advertising time within the event broadcast, presence in and around the venue, as well as use of consumer promotions and congratulatory messages" (McKelvey & Grady 2008). This definition, while more descriptive, still does not seem to encompass all the ways in which brands end up being accused of ambushing.

Types of ambushing

In an effort to summarize current behaviors, the discussion here is organized along two dimensions, intent and legality, and produces four groups:

1. intentional and illegal ambushing;
2. intentional yet not illegal ambushing activities (these are at least not illegal in an easily addressed way);
3. unintentional and legal ambushing, which is often considered incidental ambushing; and

4. unintentional and illegal ambushing (again the term ambushing is used reluctantly) where a brand, unaware of relevant laws, unintentionally violates these laws in seeking to market its products.

Intentional and illegal ambushing

The strong stand on ambushing sees the sponsor as having expended considerable money to support the event and, in turn, having some exclusive rights to associate with the event. For example, sponsors are typically allowed to use a property's logo in their own product- and service-related communications. For an ambusher to use a property's logo is to cross the line in the legal sand.

Chadwick and Burton (2011), in their categorization of the various types of ambushing, call this extreme end, "predatory ambushing." They describe it as "the deliberate ambushing of a market competitor, intentionally and knowingly attacking a rival's official sponsorship in an effort to gain market share and to confuse consumers as to who is the official sponsor" (p. 715).

One could also group any kind of property infringement in this extreme category. Here, trademark laws apply in most countries to protect a sponsoring brand. A prime example would be if a non-sponsor put the Olympic rings on their advertisement when they do not have the rights to utilize this symbol. "Passing off" or "misappropriation of one's goods, services, or commercial property as having some association or affiliation with an outside party when no such link exists" is a fallback legal protection never meant for protecting against ambushing (Burton & Chadwick 2009).

Arguably, in most countries, clearly illegal forms of ambushing are on the decline since the obvious violation of law makes little sense for the ambusher. Clever ambushers seek to avoid legal repercussions and the spelling out of what is and is not considered to be ambushing allows them to avoid violations. Intentional and illegal ambushing is most likely when enforcement of laws relied upon in prosecuting ambushers is weak. For example, despite increased awareness of ambushing in the People's Republic of China, researchers examining the frequency of ambushing there conclude, "In comparison to Western and other developed countries, the PRC, for several reasons, appears to be a country prone to ambush marketing" (Preuss et al. 2008, p. 259). The cultural reasons for this tendency are based on the Confucian tradition where sharing without restriction is valued; in addition, the scholars note an evolving understanding of sponsorship rights and related laws. Still, even in the most protective contexts, international sponsorship is complex and multilayered. When considered across countries and jurisdictions, the creative possibilities for ambushing are limitless.

Also reducing legal action, even in the face of obvious ambushing, is the fact that a body of universally accepted anti-ambushing legislation has not been developed. For example, if there is "intent to confuse" or the reasonable likelihood of blurring the ability to clearly identify a mark—the probability of causing confusion—then under the US Federal Trademark Dilution Act, the true sponsor may have a successful case. Ambush-related activities must be shown to be lessening the capacity of a famous mark to identify and distinguish goods or services, regardless of the presence or absence of (1) competition between the owner of the famous mark and other parties; or (2) likelihood of confusion, mistake, or deception. This does, however, require evidence, which can be challenging to provide in ways accepted by courts.

Another sticking point is that application of the US Federal Trademark Dilution Act is only appropriate if the mark is truly nationally famous. For example, in the case where the University of Texas sued KST Electric Limited, it was found that the former's longhorn mark was not nationally famous. The longhorn steer in silhouette was used by the university and by the electric company, but the university in their claim was only able to demonstrate "niche fame in sports", and so lost to KST (Tushnet 2008).

The true sponsor could argue that ambushing has tarnished one's brand and this too falls under trademark dilution. This aspect of trademark law termed "tarnishment" happens when a brand is portrayed in a negative light by the behavior of the other brand—for example, associated with drug use or crime. This is a stretch for the legislation and is only invoked in highly unusual circumstances. If, for example, two brands, one, a sponsor (and producer of high-quality sport shoes), were ambushed by a second brand (producing low-quality shoes), the argument could be that the two were confused by the ambushing activity but also that this confusion resulted in consumers believing that the sponsor sold inferior products. In this sense, it could be argued that the official sponsor's quality image was tarnished. This is difficult to demonstrate.

Moreover, in intentional ambushing it is likely that the brand's value in the relationship is reduced via ambushing but it is the event owner's intellectual property rights that are more likely violated. The symbols, identifying marks, or images misappropriated are likely those of the event not the brand. In this sense, ambushing is a primary concern for the property. Further, if the event is not successful in dealing with ambushing effectively, the future value of their rights may be lessened.

Intentional and legal: Ambushing as creative strategy

Somewhat against the tide of anti-ambushing, Tony Meenaghan (1996) was one of the first to argue that ambushing is a legitimate marketing activity.

He claimed that marketers have every right to use all opportunities at their disposal, including the fact that many countries protect commercial speech, to compete in the marketplace. Going one step further, to make it illegal for all marketers, save those officially sanctioned by the event and the venue, to communicate with their potential audiences in this context could be viewed as overly restrictive.

Thus, what some call "associative ambushing," others might call clever marketing. It is described as "the use of imagery or terminology to create an allusion that an organization has links to a sporting event or property, without making any specific references or implying an official association with the property" (Chadwick & Burton 2011, p. 716). Viewers of swimming events during the 2012 London Olympics might recall seeing athletes wearing headphones that sported an argyle-like British flag pattern. The company behind the headphones giveaway and their inspired appearance poolside was Beats Electronics. The brand was not an official sponsor and was seen by the International Olympic Committee as ambushing, although their approach never crossed the somewhat imaginary line. Beats had given away products during the 2008 Olympic Games but did not face the same reaction as in 2012. In this example, just seeing the product in use at a venue allowed audiences to draw an association between the event and the brand.

Even further from charges of illegality are the various strategies that employ some official connection with an event but utilize this connection in a way that may be perceived as undermining an official sponsor. For example, intensive leveraging of a low-tier sponsorship (Burton & Chadwick 2009) is thought of as ambushing since it can give one the impression of being an official partner. It has been shown to be a widely employed strategy, at least in print advertising (Kelly et al. 2012). Another cost savings approach is to sponsor the event at a high level such as title sponsor, and then reduce sponsorship level and cost in subsequent years. This cannot be viewed as an illegal strategy but works like ambushing by capitalizing on the carry over effects of having once been title sponsor.

No marketer is more associated with clever "ambushing" than sport brand Nike. Beginning in 1996, with their marketing communications surrounding the Atlanta Olympic Games, Nike has perfected dancing along the line in the sand between legal and illegal without generally tipping over it. Take, for example, their viral video entitled "Write the Future" which connected with the 2010 South African World Cup where adidas was the official sponsor. The award-winning three-minute film produced by agency Wieden & Kennedy features Cristiano Ronaldo, Wayne Rooney, and Franck Ribery doing the dazzling work of elite, Nike-sponsored athletes (Diaz 2011). This video, downloaded by millions, along with other individual and team sponsorships resulted in their being, on some measures, the brand most identified with the 2010 World Cup (Nielsen 2010). While more discussion of the nature and depth of this association is needed, there really is no disagreement about the fact that Nike successfully linked to the World Cup games without being the official FIFA partner. Carrying this success forward, in advance of 2014 World Cup play, Brazilians more strongly associate Nike with the event than official sponsor adidas (*Sports Business Daily Global Journal* 2012).

It should be emphasized that the investment to sponsor a world-class event is unequivocally more than the cost to ambush it. Take, for example, the 2006 ambushing of the FIFA World Cup sponsor Emirates Airline by German-based Lufthansa. The ambush involved putting decals on the nosecones of 40 Lufthansa aircraft (Wilson 2006) so that they looked like classic footballs with black and white hexagons. Just as an approximation, the Emirates sponsorship with FIFA that was signed in 2006 was estimated to be worth $195 million for the upcoming eight years. The cost to paint 40 nosecones was far less, and the connectivity to the event was also different, yet the public discussion of the ambushing makes it a noteworthy example even today.

Unintentional and legal: Incidental ambushing

We must also say that some brands may be "incidental" ambushers (Quester 1997). In her study of the 1994 Adelaide Formula One Grand Prix in Australia, Quester was the first to note that some brands were thought to be sponsors despite their having no premeditated intent to associate with the event. More broadly, incidental ambushing brands, in a test of recall or recognition of sponsors, may better the memory for true sponsors simply because they match well with the event. They might also score well in a memory test for sponsors of an event because they sponsor something similar or have even sponsored this event in the past. Likewise, they might accrue positive image and attitude values from being believed to be a sponsor. There is only antidotal evidence currently available that attests to this but no extensive research.

Unintentional and illegal: Unwitting "ambushers"

A fourth category might arise where a brand unintentionally violates laws in seeking to market its products through some association with the pro-tected event. This might seem to be a small or even unlikely group but as sponsorship laws expand, more and more unwary marketers and advertisers blunder into or challenge this category of accidental ambushers. Small businesses that use trademark protected terms or symbols can unwittingly fall afoul of law. They can, of course, also challenge it by what they would argue is not ambushing but within their purview as businesspeople in a context where there is a protected sponsor. No finer example of this can be found than when the Olympics are in town. The London Olympic Games Organizing Committee (LOGOC) put forward a definition of advertising that is so comprehensive yet broad to be called a "right of association" (Scassa 2011). Under this law a local florist's window display of flowers in the shape and colors of the Olympic rings could be against the law if there is any reason to suspect that they are participating in an ambush marketing campaign.

This larger net has caught many unsuspecting marketers. Take, for example, Raverly, a web-based knitting community. The group's "Ravelympics" event is where "thousands of knitters attempt to complete an ambitious project—such as knitting a hat for the first time, or finishing an entire blanket—during the two weeks the official Olympic Games take place. They form teams and challenge each other to events such as "scarf hockey" and "sock put" (Suddath 2012). Feeling that the event denigrates the true nature of the Olympic Games, the US Olympic Committee sent the 2 million knitters a cease-and-desist letter (Suddath 2012). It should be noted that the USOC has particular rights under the Ted Stevens Olympic and Amateur Sports Act of 1998, such that the USOC can stop the use of marks by others without having to prove consumer confusion as is typical in trademark infringement generally. There is an increasing interest in these accidental ambushers and call for balance between protection for rights holders and freedom of speech, as well as meaningful community engagement with exciting events (Cooper 2008).

If we take a broader view of the situation, sponsorship of events creates an out-group of advertisers that seek to associate with the event. These out-groups are now extensive since any brand not officially supporting an event is a potential ambusher. A few decades ago, before sponsorship became commonplace, to align with events was considered by advertisers to be a "use the news" strategy. For example, in the 1980s after the Boston Marathon, an advertisement for pain relief could say "if you ran in the race yesterday, you may need us today" and not be thought of as an ambusher. This then takes us full circle in terms of protecting sponsors and opens the question of where sponsors' rights conflict with the rights of others.

Ambushing at a distance

The emphasis on ambushing has tended to center on the actions surrounding the event but recent research suggests ambushing at a distance via advertising is also possible (Kelly et al. 2012). Moreover, this sort of ambushing may reach an even larger audience than those at the event. Because evidence of ambushing at a distance would be challenging to examine in a court of law, Kelly et al. (2012) devised a three-point test of intent. After considering the theme of the advertising, and establishing that there is an official sponsor in a product category, and the advertised brand's status as sponsor or non-sponsor, the following were considered:

1. timing of the ad placement (close proximity to the event);
2. context of the placement (in the instance of this study, ads were in the same magazine as that of the true sponsor); and
3. press coverage of competitive intensity (media attention about the competition in the category or even of possible ambushing).

Their studies of hundreds of print advertisements found many true sponsors with sponsorship-linked advertising that is either thematically tied to a sponsored event or at the minimum "tagged" with a logo indicating, for instance, their "proud sponsorship" status. Many brands in the same product category as the true sponsor did, however, show some intent to ambush according to the three-point test. Ambushing stemmed from the use of visuals, or wording to associate with an event, but none actually misappropriated logos.

Protection against ambushing

There is no end of advice on how to avoid ambushing (McKelvey & Grady 2008; Payne 1998; Pitt et al. 2010). Early discussions about ambushing focused on the importance of exclusivity (Payne 1998). Michael Payne, from the International Olympic Committee, argued that the process of clearly identifying rights to be included in a sponsorship package had to involve, in the case of the Olympics, rights to the event, rights to the international federation, rights to the national team, rights to the athletes, and clearly delineating any rights these parties *do not* have. This aspect of sponsoring, exclusivity, has become key in any contract.

McKelvey and Grady (2008) divide the ambushing protection strategies into four groups.

1. *Pre-event education and public relations initiatives* that are largely oriented toward event organizers (e.g., World Cup, Cricket World Cup) and seek to develop an understanding in advance about the differences between an official sponsor and an ambusher. This strategy is also presumably directed to consumers or event attendees but individuals typically do not care about making this distinction (e.g., Shani & Sandler 1998).

2. *On-site policing and establishment of "clean zones,"* where other brands are excluded. This can involve covering up logos and signs, patrolling areas, buying up available advertising spaces, controlling access to events and hospitality, and getting municipal or other government support in these efforts.

Many of these activities come with the risk of backlash by fans and other marketers that feel their rights are being violated. A notable case of policing policies with repercussions was the official response to the Dutch beer company Bavaria NV (*Datamonitor* 2010). At the 2010 World Cup in South Africa the official beer sponsor was Budweiser. Bavaria sent more than 30 women dressed in identical orange dresses to the Netherlands–Denmark match. The color orange is the color of the Dutch royal family and the color of the Netherlands national team. Without branding on the dresses, the patrolling ambush police might not have been tipped off but Bavaria had done something similar at the 2006 World Cup in Germany. There, hundreds of fans wearing Bavaria-branded orange lederhosen were forced to take their pants off by the FIFA representatives. The marketers behind the Bavaria brand had been careful not to use their brand in 2010 and thus, when the women were detained, it garnered even more media attention. Bavaria gained worldwide media coverage in part due to FIFA's decision to detain the women.

Another proactive protection strategy is the development of clean zones. Clean zones that allow only officially authorized vendors and prohibit display of unauthorized signs and banners can go well beyond established local laws. Grandiose rights have been scaled down in some cases. At the 2013 Super Bowl game in New Orleans, the size of the clean zone was reduced after a lawsuit posed by the American Civil Liberties Union of Louisiana.

3. *Specific use of contractual language* and, further, participant agreements limiting ambushing. McKelvey and Grady (2008) point out that contractual prohibitions for both athletes, who might have other sponsor relationships, and spectators, who might display signage or in some way distribute promotional materials, are new areas of control. These measures are being added to the already extensive ambush prevention requirements negotiated with most host cities for large events.

One of the most memorable participant ambushing stunts that no doubt contributed to the legislative changes over the past decades was that of sprinter Linford Christie. At the 1996 Olympic Games in Atlanta, Georgia, when Reebok was the official sponsor, he attended a press conference wearing contact lenses that featured the Puma logo. Needless to say, it made for a great photo and was shown worldwide the next day.

4. *Enactment and enforcement of trademark protection legislation* that protects words, symbols, and images that are associated with the event. The typical approach is to list those things to be protected, to communicate them to any would-be marketer or retailer in advance of the event, and to engage the host venue in protection. As an example, the International Olympic Committee prepares the "Technical Manual on Brand Protection," a 100-plus-page document, to clarify what is to be protected by the host city and the Olympic Games/Paralympic Games Advertising and Trading Regulations.

In addition to legal instruction, one can add some practical advice. From the perspective of the sponsor, Pitt et al. (2010) suggest that one cannot rely on the property, the government, or the legal system for ambushing guidance or protection. Following their analysis of the 2008 Beijing Olympics, they point out that the property has other important things to do and, given the huge number of sponsors for a large event (63 in Beijing), they are usually busy. Moreover, governments and legal systems have a hard time applying intellectual property rights, which were originally designed for other purposes, to myriad ambushing tactics.

There are also views on the appropriateness and morality of ambushing. As mentioned, at one end of the continuum some consider it an unethical business practice, while at the other end it is seen as clever and entertaining marketing antics that cause no harm. The unethical or improper nature of some marketing activities delves into social norms—what *should* be done. O'Sullivan and Murphy (1998) have argued that there needs to be an international code of conduct for event sponsorship. Many large events have codes but, to date, no standard or unified code of conduct has been developed. In making ethical decisions O'Sullivan and Murphy suggest that four ideals should be brought to bear: justice, equality, freedom, and truth (1998, p. 359). Being truthful and just in dealings is straightforward, at least in theory. The ideas of equality and freedom take particular meaning in ambushing. The large and the powerful should not be able to limit freedom of speech and expression regarding events and activities in society. Some would say that pendulum swung toward protection of the sponsor up until the 2012 London Olympic Games but given the backlash of public discourse around overly restrictive communication policies for the event, it has swung back towards freedom of speech.

As a final thought, the idea of "corporate citizenship" expands our understanding of the corporation as having individual rights (cf. Matten & Crane 2005) we also must emphasize the corporate citizen's responsibilities. The global nature of many high-profile events means that these events are not tied to any one nation, thus making the ethical behavior of boundary-spanning organizations and corporations all the more important.

Counter-ambushing

What is a firm to do if it is ambushed? Further, what will be the result of any counter-ambushing communications and strategies? Event organizers are often contractually responsible to the sponsors to wage counter-ambush strategies. A heavy-handed approach, relying upon legislation, may be supported in extreme cases of ambushing, but historically there has been reluctance for sponsoring brands to take this line of attack, presumably for fear of a backlash in the form of negative publicity (McKelvey & Grady 2008).

It is also possible for true sponsors to "name and shame" ambushing brands. A communication effort of this type presumes some level of understanding and concern about the practice of ambushing. It also assumes that if individuals know that one brand is the true sponsor and another an ambusher, that when revealed, positive associations will flow to the sponsor and negative associations to the ambusher. This argument has been supported in studies where individuals were asked about their perceptions of ambushing. These studies, however, focus on the topic and ask questions such as "Companies that associate with the NYC Marathon without being an official sponsor are being unethical" and "Companies that are not official sponsors try and mislead the public into believing that they are official sponsors" (McKelvey et al. 2012, p. 12). Questioning of this type may create characteristics not found in the practice of ambushing. In reality, people may not be aware that a brand is an ambusher and if they are, they may well find the ambusher to be entertaining, rather than "bad."

Name-and-shame strategies might have other consequences. Pitt et al. (2010) have suggested that if the true sponsor lashes out at the ambusher in a public statement, they run the risk of being considered a bully. From a communications perspective, counter-attacks may attract extra attention to the ambusher. In terms of memory for the event and its sponsors, this could be particularly detrimental if, over time, the ambusher is better remembered in association with the event than the true sponsor.

Humphreys et al. (2010) examined the influence of ambushing in a lab setting via several experiments. Their studies showed that even over a few days, information about an ambusher when a counter-ambushing strategy is employed is able to cement the relationship between the event and the ambushing brand in the mind of the consumer. These findings suggest that a heavy-handed approach, including counter-ambushing messages, especially around the time of the event, may well backfire and create memory for the ambusher.

Counterintuitive thinking about ambushing

Although it might seem strange, there can be situations where an ambusher might not be so terrible. The presence of a competitor or ambusher might even support memory for the true sponsor—when particular conditions apply. One condition affecting sponsor memory in particular is that if an ambusher is present and a person is made to think about their role relative to the true sponsor, this supports memory as the person is likely to think about which brand is the official sponsor.

It has been shown in laboratory studies undertaken at a university, that when individuals have had exposure to a variety of sponsor–event relationships and when those exposures include a direct competitor, they can help support memory for the true sponsor (Cornwell et al. 2012). This stems from the fact that people store a great deal of information in memory and thinking about an ambusher could bring up thoughts of the true sponsor. In this process, a network of memories as being made active by either the sponsor or another product in the same category or by something at an event. If we think of memory as nodes of information with links to other nodes (Anderson & Bower 1974) then it is easy to see that thoughts of one brand or company could support thinking of another.

For example, attendees of an eight-week long Aspen, Colorado, summer music festival might sit on the lawn listening to some Berg, Bernstein, or Britten. The event is sponsored by FIJI Water (which it has been for many years), but another upscale brand of bottled water, Evian, is available for purchase near the event. When away from the event, the next week, a person might be confused about which bottled water company sponsored the event because both were present in one way or another during this time. Alternatively, if the Aspen Music Festival surveyed event attendees about non-sponsor Evian, this may have prompted a person to think, "We had bottles of Evian on the street, but no, the sponsor at the event was FIJI, I'm sure of that." That is, if asked, "Who was the sponsor of the Aspen Music Festival?" the presence of the other brand might have supported memory for the true sponsor through a point of contrast. This idea may seem counter-intuitive, but the following theories provide additional insight into conditions that might make this more plausible.

Prominence and relatedness biases

Brands have different reputations or brand equities in the marketplace. When individuals make inferences about who sponsored what, it is easy to infer that a well-known brand might have been the sponsor of an event. This bias due to "market prominence" refers to consumers' use of variations in the market prominence of potential sponsors as a source of information when inferring the identity of event sponsors (Pham & Johar 2001, p. 124). Research has shown that sponsor identification is biased toward brands having high market prominence (Johar & Pham 1999) so that someone is more likely to remember the top brand in a category and less likely to remember the fourth-ranking brand, even if that brand is the actual sponsor of the event. The same sort of process holds when a brand is more closely related to a sponsored property than another, which is referred to as relatedness bias.

How do these prominence and relatedness processes work in ambushing? Based on the work of Klayman & Ha (1987), Johar & Pham suggest that individuals rely on a hypothesis-testing approach where "sponsors suggested by their (possibly vague) recollection are 'cross-checked' against cues available during identification, such as prominence." For example, you might have some recollection that FIJI Water was the sponsor of the Aspen Music Festival. When surveyed about which of several brands of bottled water sponsored the event, your confidence might be bolstered by the fact that FIJI is a prominent brand, especially if the other brands listed as foils, or false answers, are small brands. On the other hand, if the other brands listed on the survey include well-established brands such as Dasani and Evian, you might pause, and think it is one of these companies unless other disconfirming information comes to mind.

In summary, this thinking suggests that large brands will likely be advantaged when small, lesser-known brands attempt to ambush them. On recollection, the prominence bias will likely support memory for the major brand. Less prominent brands will likely suffer more if a brand with greater market share ambushes. Also, competitor or ambusher information may not be overly detrimental to memory, and may in fact support it. This point about memory does not, however, inform tendencies to like or prefer the sponsoring or ambushing brand.

It would be amiss not to consider attitudes in ambushing. Positive attitude may not necessarily follow with improvements in memory. Although interrelated, memory and attitude are decidedly different. More than likely you can remember a really annoying loud repetitive advertisement but dislike it. The same may be true in sponsorship. If, for example, the audience members for an activity or event feel negatively toward the act of ambushing, they might remember the ambush but dislike the brand for behaving in this way. When people clearly understand that a brand is engaging in ambushing through some kind of disclosure, then negative attitudes may result (Mazodier & Quester 2010). In a case study of the financial services company ING, and its sponsorship of the New York City Marathon, researchers (McKelvey et al. 2012) found that participants held negative attitudes toward companies engaged in the practice of ambushing true sponsor ING.

On the other hand, individuals have a hard time distinguishing sponsors from non-sponsors whether they are ambushers or not (Shani & Sandler 1998). Motivation to support a sponsor is most likely when individuals identify with the company (Cornwell & Coote 2005) or when they feel some sense of reciprocity (Pracejus 2004). For example, the National Association of Stock Car Auto Racing (NASCAR) uses the "driver–fan–sponsor reciprocity" model in decision-making (Sutton 2007). Because NASCAR fans know that without sponsor money, their favorite team would not race, they get to know who the sponsors are and purchase from them in appreciation for the sponsors' support of the event.

Unless audiences have a reason to value the sponsor, such as their known contribution to the activity or the event that is taking place, then they have little motivation to make strong distinctions between official sponsors and ambushers. It is also the case that asking individuals about their thoughts and feelings regarding ambushing may result in a socially desirable response, indicating dislike of the activity of ambushing, but without the conviction to alter behavior to support the true sponsor or punish the ambusher.

In reviewing ambushing practice and research, one can conclude that money and effort invested in preventing ambushing, especially in areas that may result in public backlash, are probably better spent on building a strong campaign around the official sponsor's message. The occasional clever ambush does gain media attention and is price effective but full understanding of the viewer response to ambushing is elusive. On the other hand, ambushing does create spectacle and some might say has become part and parcel of event sponsoring.

References

Anderson, J. R. & Bower, G. H. (1974). A Propositional Theory of Recognition Memory. *Memory & Cognition*, 2, 3, 406–12.

Burton, N. & Chadwick, S. (2009). Ambush Marketing in Sport: An Analysis of Sponsorship Protection Means and Counter-ambush Measures. *Journal of Sponsorship*, 2, 4, 303–15.

Business Insider (2013). GM Is Spending a Lot of Money to Expand Its Production in Mexico. *Business Insider*, June 26. Retrieved November 25, 2013 from http://www.businessinsider.com/gm-invests-691-million-in-mexico-plants-2013-6.

Chadwick, S. & Burton, N. (2011). The Evolving Sophistication of Ambush Marketing: A Typology of Strategies. *Thunderbird International Business Review*, 53, 6, 709–19.

Colao, J. J. (2013). The Five Most Expensive Jersey Sponsorships in European Soccer. *Forbes*. Retrieved November 26, 2013 from http://www.forbes.com/sites/jjcolao/2013/04/22/the-five-most-expensive-jersey-sponsorships-in-european-soccer/.

Cooper, B. (2008). Balance of Rights—Getting It Right, Part 1. *Journal of Sponsorship*, *2*, 1, 85–95.

Cornwell, T. B. & Coote, L. V. (2005). Corporate Sponsorship of a Cause: The Role of Identification in Purchase Intent. *Journal of Business Research*, *58*, 3, 268–76.

Cornwell, T. B., Humphreys, M. S., Quinn, E. & McAlister, A. R. (2012). Memory of Sponsorship-linked Communications: The Effect of Competitor Mentions. *SAGE Open*, (October–December), 1–14.

Datamonitor (2010). Ambush Marketing Case Study: Successfully Leveraging High-Profile Events to Raise Brand Profile. *Datamonitor*, July (reference code: CSCM0326), 1–12.

Diaz, A.-C. (2011). Nike's "Write the Future" Scores Cannes Film Grand Prix. *Advertising Age*, June 25. Retrieved August 21, 2013 from http://adage.com/article/special-report-cannes/cannes-film-grand-prix-nike-s-write-future/228432/.

Humphreys, M. S., Cornwell, T. B., McAlister, A. R., Kelly, S. J., Quinn, E. A. & Murray, K. L. (2010). Sponsorship, Ambushing and Counter-strategy: Effects upon Memory for Sponsor and Event. *Journal of Experimental Psychology: Applied*, *16*, 1, 96–108.

Johar, G. V. & Pham, M. T. (1999). Relatedness, Prominence, and Constructive Sponsor Identification. *Journal of Marketing Research*, *36*, 3, 299–312.

Kelly, S. J., Cornwell, T. B., Coote, L. V. & McAlister, A. R. (2012). Event-related Advertising and the Special Case of Sponsorship-linked Advertising. *International Journal of Advertising*, *31*, 1, 15–37.

Klayman, J. & Ha, Y. W. (1987). Confirmation, Disconfirmation and Information in Hypothesis Testing. *Psychological Review*, *94*, 211–28.

Matten, D. & Crane, A. (2005). Corporate Citizenship: Toward an Extended Theoretical Conceptualization. *Academy of Management Review*, *30*, 1, 166–79.

Mazodier, M. & Quester, P. (2010). Ambush Marketing Disclosure Impact on Attitudes toward the Ambusher's Brand. *Recherche et Applications en Marketing*, *25*, 2, 51–67.

McKelvey, S. & Grady, J. (2008). Sponsorship Program Protection Strategies for Special Sports Events: Are Event Organizers Outmaneuvering Ambush Marketers? *Journal of Sport Management*, *22*, 550–86.

McKelvey, S., Sandler, D. & Snyder, K. (2012). Sport Participant Attitudes toward Ambush Marketing: An Exploratory Study of ING New York City Marathon Runners. *Sport Marketing Quarterly*, *21*, 7–18.

Meenaghan, T. (1996). Ambush Marketing: A Threat to Corporate Sponsorship? *Sloan Management Review*, *38*, 1, 103–13.

Nielsen (2010). Nike Ambushes Official World Cup Sponsors. *Media and Entertainment*, June 11. Retrieved August 21, 2013 from http://www.nielsen.com/us/en/newswire/2010/nike-ambushes-official-world-cup-sponsors.html.

O'Sullivan, P. & Murphy, P. (1998). Ambush Marketing: The Ethical Issues. *Journal of Public Policy & Marketing*, *14*, 4, 349–66.

Payne, M. (1998). Ambush Marketing: the Undeserved Advantage. *Psychology & Marketing*, *14*, 4, 323–31.

Pham, M. T. & Johar, G. V. (2001). Market Prominence Biases in Sponsor Identification: Processes and Consequentiality. *Psychology & Marketing*, *18*, 2, 123–43.

Phelps, M. (2013). Personal Communication, December 5, 2013.

Pitt, L., Parent, M., Berthon, P. & Steyn, P. G. (2010). Event Sponsorship and Ambush Marketing: Lessons from the Beijing Olympics. *Business Horizons, 53,* 281–90.

Pracejus, J. W. (2004). Seven Psychological Mechanisms Through Which Sponsorship Can Influence Consumers. In L. R. Kahle & C. Riley (eds), *Sports Marketing and the Psychology of Marketing Communications,* pp. 175–90. Mahwah, NJ: Lawrence Erlbaum Associates.

Preuss, H., Gemeinder, K. & Séguin, B. (2008). Ambush Marketing in China: Counterbalancing Olympic Sponsorship Efforts. *Asian Business & Management, 7,* 243–63.

Quester, P. (1997). Awareness as a Measure of Sponsorship Effectiveness: The Adelaide Formula One Grand Prix and Evidence of Incidental Ambush Effects. *Journal of Marketing Communications, 3,* 2, 1–20.

Sandler, D. M. & Shani, D. (1989). Olympic Sponsorship vs "Ambush" Marketing: Who Gets the Gold? *Journal of Advertising Research, 29,* 4, 9–14.

Scassa, T. (2011). Ambush Marketing and the Right of Association: Clamping Down on References to That Big Event with All the Athletes in a Couple of Years. *Journal of Sport Management, 25,* 354–70.

Shani, D. & Sandler, D. M. (1998). Ambush Marketing: Is Confusion to Blame for the Flickering of the Flame? *Psychology and Marketing, 15,* 4, 367–83.

Sharma, R. (2012). Pants Joker Bendtner Banned and Fined £80k (That's £64,000 More Than Porto Faced for Racism against Balotelli). *MailOnline,* June 18. Retrieved October 26, 2013 from http://www.dailymail.co.uk/sport/euro 2012/article-2161082/Euro-2012-Nicklas-Bendtner-fined-80k-banned-UEFA-showing-pants.html.

Sports Business Daily Global Journal (2012). Nike Is Brand Most Associated With 2014 World Cup Amongst Brazilians. *Sports Business Daily Global Journal,* June 22. Retrieved August 21, 2013 from http://www.sportsbusinessdaily.com/Global/Issues/2012/06/22/Marketing-and-Sponsorship/Nike.aspx.

Suddath, C. (2012). Why the U.S. Olympic Committee Cracked Down on a Knitting Group. *Bloomberg Businessweek,* June 22. Retrieved August 21, 2013 from http://www.businessweek.com/articles/2012-06-22/why-the-u-dot-s-dot-olympic-committee-cracked-down-on-a-knitting-group.

Sutton, B. (2007). NASCAR Model Uses Driver-Fan-Sponsor Reciprocity for Success. *Sports Business Journal,* September 24. Retrieved August 20, 2013 from http://www.sportsbusinessdaily.com/Journal/Issues/2007/09/20070924/From-The-Field-Of/NASCAR-Model-Uses-Driver-Fan-Sponsor-Reciprocity-For-Success.aspx.

Townley, S., Harrington, D. & Couchman, N. (1998). The Legal and Practical Prevention of Ambush Marketing in Sports. *Psychology and Marketing, 15,* 333–48.

Tushnet, R. (2008). Longhorn Is Long Shot for Federal Fame. Retrieved December 27, 2013 from http://tushnet.blogspot.com/2008/03/longhorn-is-long-shot-for-federal-fame.html.

Wilson, B. (2006). Protecting Sport Sponsors from Ambush. *BBC News.* Retrieved November 27, 2013 from news.bbc.co.uk/2/hi/business/4719368.stm.

10

RELATIONSHIPS—BEGINNING, MANAGING, AND ENDING

Energy Australia, an electricity and gas provider headquartered in Melbourne, signed a five-year agreement in February 2012 to be the principal partner of Swimming Australia, but in June 2013, the firm ended their agreement to sponsor the sport (Balym 2013). Poor performance in the pool at the 2012 Olympic Games was only part of the picture. Salary disputes, leaked documents of lewd behavior on the part of the head coach, and "obnoxious" behavior on the part of swimmers led an independent reviewer from the Australian Sports Commission to label the team's culture as "toxic" (Balym 2013).

A good deal of thinking has been put into starting sponsorship relationships. Much of this is accounted for in discussions of prospecting on the part of the property and proposal evaluation on the part of the sponsor. Far less is written about the challenges of managing sponsorship relationships and even less has been written about ending them. In sponsorship, understanding the ending of relationships is decidedly important for at least two reasons. First, as a departing sponsor, the legacy of sponsoring carries forward beyond the end of the contractual relationship. Breaking a sponsorship contract may appear as abandoning a group in need or as the only appropriate response to a toxic situation depending in part on how the break up is managed. Second, as one sponsorship ends, another typically begins and to take over a property, whether one with a questionable or a glorious past, comes with a set of associations. For a future sponsor, one important consideration is the set of associations that may persist from any past sponsors.

The nature of sponsorship relationships

Many relationships in marketing are vertical; that is to say, they are structured as a chain of relationships involving producers, wholesalers, and retailers that result in the end product on a shelf. Vertical marketing systems are often in the same industry such as auto parts and autos. In contrast, horizontal marketing systems combine entities at the same level, and at times, across industries. For example, an airline might work with a vacation destination to create a packaged deal to offer to consumers. Sponsorship relationships can have aspects of both structures. Sport stadiums selling pouring rights to beverage sponsors have vertical relationships. A horizontal relationship in the context of sponsorship could be the combination of game play content with program development to offer a joint product.

Sponsorship relationships are, however, best described as "symbiotic," a term used here to capture non-traditional marketing where "the alliance of resources or programs between two or more independent organizations is designed to increase the market potential of each" (Adler 1966, p. 60). Original thinking about symbiotic marketing considered franchise and licensing dealings but did not imagine the full spectrum of relationship types that are now commonplace.

Employing this symbiotic marketing in sponsorship presumes that relationships are viewed as beneficial to both parties. Symbiotic marketing connections vary in time frame, proximity (arms-length or close working), number, level (organizational, functional), focus (the offering of one partner or the offerings of both), and scope at the marketing function level (ranging from joint marketing strategy to specific aspects of programs stemming from separate strategies formulated individually) (Varadarajan & Rajaratnam 1986).

It is easy to see each of these characteristics of symbiotic relationships in sponsorship and it is also possible to see some evolution in the nature of these relationships. Historically, sponsorship contracts have focused on the brand over the property, but more and more properties are seeking commitment to activation at events, in traditional marketing, and in new media, from brands to help build their offering as well.

Proximity has always varied depending on people, organizations, and their goals but there is some discussion that better results for both organizations come from closer relationships. Historically, geographical proximity has been important in supporting business networks such as those found in sponsoring (Pieters et al. 2012). It is difficult to say the extent to which technologically enhanced communications can overcome physical distance but ties between sports, the arts, causes, and communities are logically still stronger when in close association.

Finally, the scope of sponsorship is also evolving from decidedly dedicated only to awareness building or image change to include more joint marketing and mutually beneficial platforms. A good example of collaboration is the Barclaycard Wireless Festival in 2012. This festival based in England was billed as the first music event to be fully contactless enabled—in short—without the use of currency. This was accomplished with the Barclay PayBand, a product that allowed festivalgoers to pay for everything through a near-field payment system—with the individual's details stored and worn as a bracelet (Lowe 2012). It provided a single payment system for festival vendors and unique product experiences to attendees.

Beginning new sponsorship relationships

A repeated theme in sponsoring is the movement from transaction-based thinking to relationships (Cousens et al. 2006; Farrelly 2010; Nufer & Bühler 2010) or even networks (Cobbs 2011; Ryan & Fahy 2012). The health of sponsorship relationships depends on aspects that are commonplace to other types of relationships, such as trust, mutual understanding, a long-term commitment, communication, and cooperation (Nufer & Bühler 2010). Sponsorship does, however, have relational aspects particular to the context. For example, Farrelly & Quester (2005) find that not surprisingly, trust is important to both economic and non-economic satisfaction with a sponsorship. However, commitment, as measured by leverage investment on the part of the sponsor, is important to economic satisfaction with the relationship. The importance of leveraging can be seen as a move toward a new focus in a symbiotic relationship where brand leveraging brings value to the property.

Researchers in sport management (Cousens et al. 2006) suggest that the beginning of a relationship starts with a contextual audit on the part of both the property and the corporate partner to assess the needs of the individual organizations. After the audits are complete, there is a better informational base for negotiation of the relationship benefits, management, and evaluation.

In addition to the information already available when starting new sponsorship relationships, one more fact that should be taken into consideration is that beginning a new partnership increasingly means taking over a relationship that was previously held by another sponsor. Herein lies the challenge: almost every major property today has had a prior sponsor and this creates a challenge to the new sponsor to establish memory for the relationship.

New to you

Taking a sponsorship relationship over from another sponsor should come with some consideration of the past partner for the property, particularly if the previous relationship was from the same industry. Through field surveys and experimental work, we have learned that the previous sponsor may be spontaneously recovered from memory even after a new sponsor has held the sponsorship for years. How does this happen?

A case study of Gunston cigarettes, a South African tobacco company that participated in sponsorship, provides an example. After having sponsored the Gunston 500 surfing competition for 30 years, anti-tobacco legislation forced the sponsorship relationship to end, and the event was picked up by the Mr. Price clothing retailer and renamed the Mr. Price Pro (Mason & Cochetel 2006). Although the Mr. Price brand had previous associations with surfing and a dedicated surfing line of clothes, and the Gunston sponsorship had ended two years prior to the research study, 87% of the 208 respondents had unaided recall of the previous title event sponsor, Gunston. The researchers concluded: "a new sponsor, when taking over from a long running sponsorship, needs to break the old link and establish a new strong link between the new sponsor and event (Mason & Cochetel 2006, p. 138).

The role of spontaneous recovery

Spontaneous recovery is a well-researched phenomenon in psychology (Brown 1976; Wheeler 1995). It hinges on the fact that people utilize contexts they have experienced to remember things. The old sponsor, especially if they held the sponsorship relationship for many years, has a great deal of connectivity to all the associations of the property. The old sponsor may be pictured in the mind of those visiting the venues, with players, and in advertising. Reliance on these evolving contexts and mental representations results in the "coming to mind" of the old sponsor.

In a series of field studies across four events (a tennis tournament, an auto racing event, a horse racing event, and an Olympic Games broadcast), McAlister et al. (2012) considered how well individuals remembered the new sponsor both at the time of the event and six months later. Around the time of the event, recall of the new sponsor is typically good or building, and mistaken recall of the old sponsor, while still common, is relatively low.

Across time, the recall pattern changes (in this case six months). For example, in the auto racing study, the former sponsor held the event from 2003–7 and the replacing sponsor entered with a contract in 2008. At the time of the event and the first data collection in the first year of the replacing sponsor, recall for the new sponsor was 20% and mistaken recall of the old sponsor was 23%. This is understandable since the old sponsor had been in place for five years. Six months after the event, when media attention was largely gone, recall for the new, replacing sponsor dropped to 12% while mistaken recall for the old sponsor rose to 40%.

Looking across the four events, each with a memory measure taken at the time of the event and six months from each event, Figure 10.1 shows a dramatic recovery of the old sponsor. At the time of the event, all that is happening, including information about the most recent sponsor, supports memory. After six months, all the mental connections to the old sponsor allow this relationship to come to mind and be reported as the current sponsor. Notable, is the fact that some sponsors had been replaced several years ago but were still remembered.

These findings suggest that sponsors taking over an event need to be aware of spontaneous recovery. Even if the event is new to a brand or company, this does not mean that the history of the sponsorship is no longer relevant. Emphasis in this research was not focused on the differences between those taking over from a direct competitor and those taking over from a competitor in another industry. One can, however, imagine that if a brand takes over from a direct competitor, it is only reasonable to expect significant amounts of spontaneous recovery of the previous sponsor's name.

Examples abound where competitors in the same industry take over from one another, such as when Visa took over World Cup soccer from Mastercard (Mickle 2013), when Anheuser-Busch took over the NFL league level sponsorship from MillerCoors (Lefton 2010), when PowerAde replaced Gatorade as official sports drink of major league lacrosse (Smith 2011), when Honda replaced Chevrolet as auto sponsor of the singing show competition

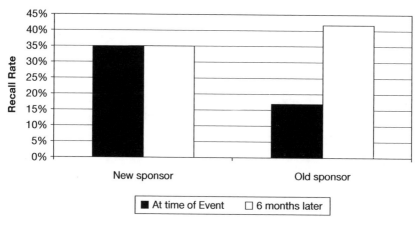

FIGURE 10.1 Spontaneous recovery research summary

Source: Based on research presented in McAlister et al. (2012).

the "X Factor" (Friedman 2013). Naturally, there are many reasons to take over from a direct competitor—to acquire a valued property, to gain distribution at the venue, to block competitors—but the extent of spontaneous recovery should be considered in balancing the value when the property has been held for many years.

Strategies to avoid spontaneous recovery would include avoiding taking over an event sponsorship from a direct competitor unless there are significant offsetting advantages. Also, communications during the off-period of an event might be valuable—an extended lead-up and clever post-event communications can extend coverage and reduce spontaneous recovery of the previous sponsor. Importantly, the spontaneous recovery phenomenon also suggests that sponsorship managers should not simply "rebadge" existing activation strategies with their corporate colors and logo. Properties typically have a slate of assets: in-net signage at tennis matches, half-time giveaways at basketball games, artist receptions at a cultural event, and corporate branded fan zones at baseball games. When these assets are utilized in exactly the same way by a new sponsor, especially a direct competitor, the potential to confuse increases.

Managing existing relationships

The importance of being involved

In an early longitudinal study of sponsorship management (Cornwell et al. 2001), the development of brand equity was linked to active management involvement. In this study, the researchers developed a management index consisting of points for: an established corporate policy, formalized sponsorship evaluation method, active over passive evaluation methods, sponsor-initiated over sponsee-initiated relationships, and extent of the sponsorship portfolio. Higher points on the index reflect more active and involved management of sponsorship and are associated with being able to differentiate the brand from competitors and the ability to add financial value to the brand. Although this research was conducted before the rapid development of sponsorship-related intermediaries and their more sophisticated support of sponsorship management, the basic thinking still holds. Managers uninvolved in their sponsorships run the risk of not achieving their full potential.

In terms of managing sponsorship relationships, Jed Pearsall, founder of Performance Research, has suggested that collaboration between sponsors and rights holders is key (Pearsall 2009). He argues that establishing metrics for sponsorship evaluation jointly and early increases the probability of a successful program. He further sees focus and agreement on metrics as a tool to correct problems as they arise, to involve a greater sphere of management, and ultimately to help partnerships survive.

The challenge to relationships of negative events

Sponsorships are difficult to manage in the best of situations but when an event such as negative player or celebrity behavior occurs, the management and continuation of the relationship can be threatened. Utilizing in-depth interviews, researchers from Australia found that negative player incidents in sports such as football, rugby, basketball, and cricket could negatively impact relationships and could lead to premature termination of the sponsorship agreement (Westberg et al. 2011). The outcome of a negative player experience depends on the attribution of blame to particular parties, the severity of the incident, and the extent of the media attention around the event. As is found in crisis management research, these researchers suggested that being prepared for these episodes is essential, as is open and trustworthy communication, and careful management of the media. As examples in contrast, golfer Tiger Woods was able to recover from the negative news about cheating on his wife, while cyclist Lance Armstrong was seen as having cheated on the sport by using drugs to enhance performance. Despite immense media attention around both athletes, in the end, the failure to the sport in the case of Lance Armstrong was insurmountable.

Ending relationships

One of the first studies to examine the ending of sponsorship relationships was conducted in Finland (Olkkonen & Tuominen 2008). This examination of a cultural sponsorship between the media company MTV3 and the Museum of Contemporary Art (Kiasma) investigated both negative and positive structural and situational triggers. Structural triggers such as the overall macroeconomic environment are relatively permanent, whereas situational triggers such as a breakdown in relationships are more transient. Interesting and relevant to all sponsorship contexts, the authors discuss the concept of relationship "fading," where a relationship seems to weaken and decline as possible precursor to ending (p. 204). This is played out often enough when early interest in a sponsorship meets with some difficulties and while the contract may be for several years, investment ends prematurely. For this particular cultural sponsorship case study, a multi-level analysis found that both structural and situational triggers played a role in fading and ending. Economic conditions forced change but changing objectives of the partners ended the relationship.

In the sport context, Farrelly (2010) examined the relationship-based reasons for sponsorship terminations through 24 in-depth interviews conducted over four years in Australia. Managers for leagues and clubs of Australian Rules football, basketball, and rugby were included, as were managers at sponsoring brands such as Nike, Honda, Coca-Cola, McDonald's, and Vodafone. Five important themes emerged from the analysis of these interview responses (Farrelly 2010). They are:

1. *Strategic versus tactical intent*—the clash of intent stems from philosophical differences regarding investments in sponsorship. Sponsors tended to view their investments as relationships with broad corporate and marketing objectives, whereas properties were seen as being limited by an orientation to tactics.
2. *Evolving relationships and a failure to adapt*—brands tended to redefine goals to match market opportunities and properties did not quickly align with new targets. The "sell and service the sponsorship" approach where properties only do what they have committed to does not address changing market conditions.
3. *Conflicting perceptions of contribution and the need for proof*—properties often feel that they are collaborative and do provide adequate support or measurement to sponsors. Sponsorship managers need proof in the form of data that they can take to their senior management, who often have conflicting views of the value of what the properties supply.
4. *Commitment asymmetry*—this sort of conflict arises when one party, typically the sponsor, expands its leveraging and activation associated with a property. If the property, which also gains value from sponsor leveraging, does not increase its commitment, an imbalance can result. Seemingly, perceptions of asymmetry may be as important as true asymmetry.
5. *Capability gap*—perhaps the most fundamental of the themes identified was the difference in capabilities between sponsors and properties. Farrelly (2010) writes: "Several of the sponsors we interviewed determined that properties had neither the partnering nor the sponsorship capabilities to create competitive advantage through the blending of resources" (p. 328). Further, he writes "For many of the properties we investigated, the difficulty in finding a path to collaboration was a by-product of a culture built on securing rather than managing sponsorships. (p. 328).

Reflecting on these findings, it is clear to see that the history of both the property and the sponsor, and the people who work for each organization, influence relationship maintenance. In particular, the property emphasis of selling rights for a fee is in contrast to a sponsoring company's orientation to brand development. It is also worth noting that the individuals working for sport properties typically come from work and academic backgrounds in sport, education, recreation, and kinesiology, whereas brand managers typically have a background in business and marketing.

Negative consequences of ending

There is limited research on the negative consequences of ending sponsorship relationships. It has been shown in experimental work that fan attitudes toward a sponsor that terminates a contract with a favorite team are negative, especially if the team depends heavily on the sponsor for support and if there seemed to be a good match between the sport and the sponsor (Grohs et al. 2013). Furthermore, this research, conducted in the context of soccer, shows sponsors need to worry most about negative attitudes when they terminate a long-term well-fitting relationship when there is no alternative readily available. That is, the fans will feel even more resentful towards the terminating sponsor in this scenario.

In the examination of cultural sponsorships, the ending of sponsorship relationships has been shown to negatively impact employees. Researchers looking at a case study of a theater group and a retailer have found that the developed relationship between employees of the sponsoring organization and the members of the sponsored one need to be considered when relationships end (Ryan & Blois 2010). In this case, individuals working in boundary-spanning roles between the company and property developed relationships with a psychological contract or social bond. Sponsorship managers in these roles often become a bridge of sorts between the two organizations.

In relationship-intensive roles, the sponsor's employees may feel a sense of responsibility to the theater, symphony, or art museum that their company supports. When the relationships are strong, feelings of identification and a sense of "we" may develop such that ending relationships can be distressing. It is argued that the emotional labor of boundary-spanning employees— those that must develop, implement, and end sponsorship relationships—is under-recognized (Ryan & Blois 2010).

Using balance theory where it is expected that individuals will make adjustments in their attributions to maintain a harmonious relationship (Heider 1958), researchers (Ruth & Strizhakova 2012) found that in many situations the ending of a sponsorship negatively impacts attitudes. In experimental work, they considered how the sponsor's stated motive (typically sales-oriented), duration of the sponsorship, and involvement with the event domain influence attitudes. They report that "blatantly stating that the sponsorship no longer meets the brand's sales goals, as companies frequently do, has negative effects on attitudes towards the existing brand, regardless of consumer involvement with the event domain" (Ruth & Strizhakova 2012, p. 48). In short, consumers resolve feelings of imbalance after the termination of the relationship by making negative attributions to a more sales-oriented brand. If, however, the brand was not as highly sales-oriented, then involved consumers balance their disappointment over the termination with some gratitude to the brand. It is as if they are perceived as having had a less exploitive, more genuine relationship even if now ended. Less involved consumers experience smaller rebalancing effects since they did not care so much about the sponsorship anyway.

The possibility of immediately ending a sponsorship agreement without encountering overwhelming negative consequences is very much related to the way in which the contract was written. Specific clauses may be written to protect against the property's failure to perform or deliver adequately, negative publicity associated with the event, changes in advertising and promotions laws, and cancelled events (Reed et al. 2010). Either side may have reasons for exit. It is advised that even if an exit clause was not in the contract or the situation extends beyond the wording (e.g., economic downturn), it may be worthwhile to negotiate with a property if a brand must exit. Here the hope is that the property will see that getting something, such as a reduced contract length, is better than getting nothing if the enterprise can no longer hold the sponsorship.

Foremost across the research on sponsorship relationships is the emphasis on communication and setting clearly agreed upon shared goals for the relationship. The subtext that comes from these case studies is that each side needs to invest more in understanding the other—the training of the staff, the history of the respective brands, and their past relationships. Sponsorship is a people business. Under Armour's CEO Kevin Plank repeatedly points to the importance of opening doors, talking with, and learning from people in the sports apparel industry. In discussion of his approach to celebrity endorsements he notes that deals are not just about money: "You need to find out who is on the other side of the table and whom you should be talking to. There's the athlete, of course, but sometimes a friend, a handler, or mom or dad is the key decision maker. You have to build trust and explain your story" (Plank 2012). There is no one-size-fits-all formula for relationships; there is, however, a trend toward fewer, better serviced relationships that have the potential to be long-term. The beginning point for quality relationships is mutual understanding as the foundation of appropriate expectations.

References

Adler, L. (1966). Symbiotic Marketing. *Harvard Business Review*, November–December, 59–71.

Balym, T. (2013). Sponsor Bails in Wake of New Low. *The Cairns Post*, June 6, 34.

Brown, A. S. (1976). Spontaneous Recovery in Human Learning. *Psychological Bulletin, 83*, 2, 321–8.

Cobbs, J. B. (2011). The Dynamics of Relationship Marketing in International Sponsorship Networks. *Journal of Business & Industrial Marketing, 26*, 8, 590–601.

Cornwell, T. B., Roy, D. P. & Steinard, E. A. (2001). Exploring Manager's Perceptions of the Impact of Sponsorship on Brand Equity. *Journal of Advertising, 30*, 2, 41–51.

Cousens, L., Babiak, K. & Bradish, C. L. (2006). Beyond Sponsorship: Re-framing Corporate–Sport Relationships. *Sport Management Review, 9*, 1–23.

Farrelly, F. (2010). Not Playing the Game: Why Sport Sponsorship Relationships Break Down. *Journal of Sport Management, 24*, 319–37.

Farrelly, F. J. & Quester, P. G. (2005). Examining Important Relationship Quality Constructs of the Focal Sponsorship Exchange. *Industrial Marketing Management, 32*, 211–19.

Friedman, W. (2013). Honda Drives "X Factor" as Sponsor. *MediaDailyNews*. Retrieved October 5, 2013 from http://www.mediapost.com/publications/article/208641/honda-drives-x-factor-as-sponsor.html.

Grohs, R., Kopfer, K. & Woisetschläger, D. M. (2013). An Examination of Conditions that Moderate Negative Effects of Sponsorship Terminations on Fan Attitudes toward the Former Sponsor. Proceedings of the 2013 *AMS World Marketing Congress*, Melbourne, Australia.

Heider, F. (1958). *The Psychology of Interpersonal Relations*. New York: Wiley.

Lefton, T. (2010). A-B Replacing Coors as NFL's Beer Sponsor Beginning with '11 Season. *Sports Business Daily*. Retrieved October 5, 2013 from http://www.sportsbusinessdaily.com/Daily/Issues/2010/05/Issue-161/Sponsorships-Advertising-Marketing/A-B-Replacing-Coors-As-Nfls-Beer-Sponsor-Beginning-With-11-Season.aspx.

Lowe, M. (2012). Barclaycard PayBand at Wireless 2012: We Test the "Cashless Festival" Concept. Retrieved January 2, 2014 from http://www.pocket-lint.com/news/116200-barclaycard-payband-cashless-festival-concept-at-wireless-2012-using-nfc-mastercard-paypass-contactless-payments.

Mason, R. B. & Cochetel, F. (2006). Residual Brand Awareness Following the Termination of a Long-term Event Sponsorship and the Appointment of a New Sponsor. *Journal of Marketing Communications, 12*, 2, 125–44.

McAlister, A. R., Kelly, S. J., Humphreys, M. S. & Cornwell, T. B. (2012). Change in a Sponsorship Alliance and the Communication Implications of Spontaneous Recovery. *Journal of Advertising, 41*, 1, 5–16.

Mickle, T. (2013). Visa extending World Cup Deal for Eight Years. *Sports Business Journal*, April 1. Retrieved October 5, 2013 from http://www.sportsbusinessdaily.com/Journal/Issues/2013/04/01/Marketing-and-Sponsorship/Visa-FIFA.aspx.

Nufer, G. & Bühler, A. (2010). Establishing and Maintaining Win-Win Relationships in the Sports Sponsorship Business. *Journal of Sponsorship, 3*, 2, 157–68.

Olkkonen, R. & Tuominen, P. (2008). Fading Configurations in Inter-organizational Relationships: A Case Study in the Context of Cultural Sponsorship. *Journal of Business & Industrial Marketing*, *23*, 3, 203–12.

Pearsall, J. (2009). Sponsorship Performance: What is the Role of Sponsorship Metrics in Proactively Managing the Sponsor–Property Relationship? *Journal of Sponsorship*, *3*, 2, 115–23.

Pieters, M., Knoben, J. & Pouwels, M. (2012). A Social Network Perspective on Sport Management: The Effect of Network Embeddedness on Commercial Performance of Sport Organizations. *Journal of Sport Management*, *26*, 433–44.

Plank, K. (2012). Under Armour's Founder on Learning to Leverage Celebrity Endorsements. *Harvard Business Review*, May, 45–8.

Reed, M. H., Bhargava, M. N., Gordon, J. & Kjaer, M. (2010). Terminating a Sponsorship Relationship: Conditions and Clauses. *Sponsorship Journal*, *4*, 1, 79–92.

Ruth, J. A. & Strizhakova, Y. (2010). And Now, Goodbye: Consumer Response to Sponsor Exit. *International Journal of Advertising*, *31*, 1, 39–62.

Ryan, A. & Blois, K. (2010). The Emotional Dimension of Organizational Work When Cultural Sponsorship Relationships Are Dissolved. *Journal of Marketing Management*, *26*, 7–8, 612–34.

Ryan, A. & Fahy, J. (2012). Evolving Priorities in Sponsorship: From Media Management to Network Management. *Journal of Marketing Management*, *29*, 9/10, 1132–58.

Smith, M. (2011). PowerAde bumps Gatorade from MLL Sidelines. *Sports Business Journal*, February 28. Retrieved October 5, 2013 from http://www.sportsbusiness daily.com/Journal/Issues/2011/02/28/Marketing-and-Sponsorship/Powerade-MLL.aspx.

Varadarajan, P. R. & Rajaratnam, D. (1986). Symbiotic Marketing Revisited. *Journal of Marketing*, *50*, 1, 7–17.

Westberg, K., Stavros, C. & Wilson, B. (2011). The Impact of Degenerative Episodes on the Sponsorship B2B Relationship: Implications for Brand Management. *Industrial Marketing Management*, *40*, 603–11.

Wheeler, M. A. (1995). Improvement in Recall over Time without Repeated Testing: Spontaneous Recovery Revisited. *Journal of Experimental Psychology: Learning Memory, and Cognition*, *21*, 1, 173–84.

PART III

Advanced and specialized topics

11

MEMORY FOR SPONSORSHIP RELATIONSHIPS

An online survey of over 1,000 people in the US following the 2012 Olympics found that 37% of respondents identified Nike as an Olympic sponsor but only 24% identified the true sponsor in the athletic apparel and shoe category, adidas (Wentz 2012). This is perhaps understandable given all the individual Nike-sponsored teams and athletes at the event. Still, media attention focused on the success of Nike in associating with the event without being a member of the Olympic Partners program (TOP).

In the same consumer panel, true Olympic partner Coca-Cola was identified more than rival Pepsi (47% versus 28%). Importantly, respondents were given the definition of a sponsor as an organization that provides funds or support for the Olympic Games and told that the International Olympic Committee has officially recognized and has given permission for them to use the Olympic symbol/logo. While sponsors may have a strong understanding of exclusivity, meaning that their contract with the Olympics says that they are the only brand associated with the event in their product category, clearly consumers do not.

"In one of the oddest findings, perhaps influenced by what a pervasive presence Google is in the everyday life of Internet users, 16% of respondents incorrectly identified Google as an Olympic sponsor" (Wentz 2012). Moreover, 60% of those responding that Google was a sponsor felt positive toward the company for their sponsorship. To make sense of these findings and to support memory measurement in marketing, some background on memory is helpful.

Memory measurement in sponsorship

Clearly, memory outcomes for sponsors are a key indicator of sponsorship success. Typical measures used in sponsorship include improved memory for the sponsor brand, and memory for the sponsorship relationship on the part of viewers or attendees of the music, art, or sport event. Sponsorship outcomes are also recognized in consumer behavior research as a contributor to brand perceptions (Bennett 1999) and knowledge. As individuals have experiences and interactions with a brand they develop brand knowledge. In fact, "*anything* that causes the consumer to 'experience' or be exposed to the brand has the potential to increase familiarity and awareness" (Keller 1993, p. 10; emphasis in the original writing). In keeping with this thinking, sponsorship can also contribute unique, favorable, and strong brand associations that build brand image and it is the strong brand image that supports memory through brand differentiation.

The two most frequently used measures of memory in marketing are recall and recognition. Recognizing is generally thought to be easier than recalling (Humphreys & Bain 1983). The thinking here is that recognition is based largely on a continuous source of information whereas recall is based on particular information that is likely not present. Recognition, like recall, requires retrieval of information from memory, but it does not require the retrieval of *the* response that must be made (see Humphreys et al. 1994). So a survey respondent might bring from memory a number of things that help in making a recognition decision, such as the color of a banner, the celebrity's face, or even just the temperature in the arena during the event.

Recognition is the awareness that comes seemingly automatically when one compares incoming information with memory and finds that this has been previously experienced or perceived. Recognition testing is typically found in sponsorship research when a list of true sponsors and foils are listed and respondents are asked to identify which from the list were sponsors of an event. It is easy to see how "plausible" candidates might be selected as sponsors (even when not) through this process.

Recall is the process of retrieving information from memory and is thought to require both search for relevant information and choice or decision-making about what is the correct or useful information from what has been retrieved in one's mind. Recall in sponsorship usually takes the form of cued recall (or aided recall, see, for example, Lardinoit & Derbaix 2001), where the respondent can be asked to produce the event, the sponsor's name, or both. In this situation, a person must find a unique response to a researcher's question. If the particular beer sponsor of a Canadian hockey event is what is sought, then the only answer that is counted as correct is Molson.

How a question is asked is very much related to the answers one gets. In memory research the important difference in questioning lies in the cues for remembering. One study that specifically considered the variation in cueing was undertaken by Tripodi et al. (2003). Using telephone survey data collected around the time of the 2000 Olympics, they considered four approaches to measuring recall (p. 447): (1) event sponsorship prompt ("When you think of [Event Z], which sponsors come to mind?"); (2) brand sponsorship prompt ("When you think of [Brand X], what sponsorships come to mind?"); (3) category sponsorship prompt ("When you think of [Category Y, e.g., bands] what sponsorships come to mind?"); and (4) brand recognition recall ("I am going to tell you some of Brand X's current or recent sponsorships. For each one, could you tell me whether you were aware, before today, of Brand X sponsoring that event?").

Not surprisingly, Tripodi et al. found that these different approaches to measurement yielded different estimates of memory. A total of 32% of people in the "event sponsorship prompt" group recalled the target bank sponsor, Westpac, while only 16% of people in the "brand sponsorship prompt" group recalled the event when cued. The recognition prompt further supported memory for the correct sponsor, particularly for those in the "brand sponsorship prompt" group (49%). The bank sponsor of interest in the study had several larger competitors known to sponsor sport so this may have influenced the findings. While the authors could not say conclusively if the other banks' associations with sport interfered with memory of the target bank, it is plausible.

Sponsorship memory objectives

It has been argued that recall and recognition as memory objectives in sponsorship set a high hurdle (Cornwell & Humphreys 2013). Typically, event participants or survey respondents are asked to explicitly remember the link between the event property and the sponsoring brand. Imagine for a moment this standard applied to advertising. Did you learn about the new iPhone online or was it in an online news story about technology? Importantly, does it matter to the consumer?

There are times when it is important that a person can remember both the brand and the context for learning about the brand. For example, if the brand seeks to develop associations to a cause or charity in order to build its corporate social responsibility record, explicit memory of the sponsor–event relationship may be key. The brand may have a goal to be known as sponsor of the event.

In some other areas of sponsorship, this demanding level of memory may be more than is needed to further marketing-related goals. For example, in-store displays of a product may cue behavior regardless of whether or not they come with recall or recognition of the individual's most recent sponsor–event exposure. The focus of most memory research in sponsorship has been on explicit memory measured by recall and recognition of sponsors. We know much less about the memories that may be cued by an in-store context, packaging, a spokesperson, or even something as subtle as color or design. In short, we know much less about the role of implicit memory.

Explicit and implicit memory

One distinction between explicit and implicit memory is that testing for explicit memory makes reference to a particular learning episode whereas testing for implicit memory does not. An explicit memory question might ask after an event, "Do you remember seeing the logo for a sports drink during the cricket match?" An implicit measure might ask study participants to complete the stem of various words with, for example, "GA_____" or "VO____" provided as prompts for sponsoring brands Gatorade or Vodafone. In fact, these sorts of implicit measures are not new to marketing (Duke & Carlson 1994) but they are perhaps under-utilized in sponsorship research.

This distinction between explicit and implicit memory can further be thought of as the difference between the "conscious recollection of recently presented information, as expressed on traditional tests of free recall, cued recall and recognition" as compared to the facilitation of some task that is "attributable to information acquired during a previous study episode" (Schacter 1987, p. 501). For example, researchers examining memory effects of tennis spectators found that even when sponsoring brands were not recognized, they still were present more often in a consumer's consideration set (Herrmann et al. 2011). That is to say, even though they did not have explicit memory about the sponsorship relationship, their implicit memory for a sponsor "facilitated" the development of a consideration set (a subset of products in a category from which a person will choose) where the sponsor was included.

There is strategic value to memory even if memory for the relationship between the sponsor and event is not strong enough to pass the high hurdle of explicit recall. It is possible that links formed while watching or attending the event might still influence behavior. For example, someone attending the 2014 Commonwealth multi-sport games in Glasgow, Scotland, might have exposure to their sponsor, computer company Dell. Perhaps there is a glimpse of Dell's computers in use across various venues at the event, or perhaps one learns of Dell's Scottish headquarters in Dennistoun. While a person might not have a direct recollection of the event or even the performance demonstration, there could be facilitation of a brand-related task such as deciding which brand of computer to buy on a subsequent purchase occasion.

The mere exposure effect is another example where facilitation of sponsor goals may occur under limited explicit memory (Zajonc 1968). Here, repetition tends to build positive effect that we measure as liking. Learning more about this phenomenon, we find a two-step process where exposure to a stimulus leads to greater fluency in memory recall on a second exposure and this feeling of fluency or ease of recall is reported as liking (Reber et al. 1998). The idea is that enhanced fluency may not be correctly attributed to the prior exposure but rather misattributed to the brand or its characteristics. Facilitation of some action or behavior without conscious recollection is another aspect of implicit memory. This facilitation, or what we call "weak" memory objectives, has not been the focus of the majority of sponsorship research (Cornwell & Humphreys 2013).

Competitive interference

A host of variables could intervene and alter, distort, or limit the intended communications of a sponsor. Clearly one has to consider the nature of competitive activities intended as ambushing, but also important is interference from other brands in memory or in the context of exposure. Study after study shows that consumers commonly identify foils, or non-sponsors, as sponsors (e.g., Johar et al. 2006; Quester 1997) and this is disconcerting to true sponsors that have paid for an association with the event.

The good news for sponsors is that even when there may be a benefit for a competitor who is thought to be a sponsor, this may not be damaging to the true sponsor, especially if the true sponsor has developed a strong link to the event. For example, in highly controlled experiments utilizing real brand names but fictitious events, interference from competitors was rather low when the true sponsor was mentioned more frequently than the competitor brand (Cornwell et al. 2006). Thus, a well-established relationship between the true sponsor and the event may persist even if there is confusion on a test with non-sponsors.

Current context and prior knowledge

One concern in trying to measure memory effects is the fact that context likely influences most retrieval in field studies where spectators and event attendees are pre- or post-event study participants. Take, for example, a study conducted at a stadium before or after a game. Individuals are known to have more accurate memory when their "study context" or the situation surrounding learning of information is the same as their "test context." Even if researchers are careful not to have sponsor logos and advertisements visible when surveys are answered in a stadium, study participants are still cognizant of their location, including sounds, smells, and even their fellow participants' clothing, all of which could offer context cues. Research allowing strong context cues will likely show stronger recall than those studies designed to avoid context effects. This facilitated recall is, however, typically against the strong memory objective of explicit recall or recognition. Nonetheless, when posed in an alternative context—at home, online, in a store—awareness measures might yield a very different picture of memory for sponsors.

In addition, prior knowledge is typically not accounted for adequately in research on memory for sponsors. Without information on past exposures both to the sponsoring brand and to the property sponsored, we know little of how consumers make use of the current or prior experiences in recall or recognition. For example, consumer knowledge about sports events in the areas of golf, the Olympics, and basketball resulted in different perceptions of congruence between a sponsor and a sport event (Roy & Cornwell 2004). In particular, high-knowledge event experts perceived less congruence between sponsors and events than novices. Their past learning about an event such as professional golf gave them confidence in their knowledge about the types of brands that would sponsor these events.

Another way to see the influence of prior knowledge is in the heuristics, or mental short cuts, individuals use when making sense of their environment. In research on memory for sponsorship relationships, researchers have argued that individuals naturally employ a representativeness heuristic (Kahneman & Tversky 1973) to identify sponsors (Johar & Pham 1999). The logic is that when individuals seek to identify sponsors for an event, they rely partly on overlap between features of the event and those of potential sponsors. Thus, the higher the overlap, the more likely that event sponsorship will be attributed to a particular sponsor. Naturally, those individuals with more past experiences with the sponsor brand and with the event property may have stored more and more varied features than those with little past experience. This explains why Nike makes such a strong match in people's minds for so many sporting events, even when they are not the major sponsor or not even a sponsor at all.

In all memory research, it is important to be cognizant that the categories and labels that researchers use may have no meaning or relevance to those attending. Why should a person watching the Olympics be aware of the fact or care that the TOP sponsors have exclusive rights in a category? Why should individuals be offended or indignant about ambushing when it is creative and fun? Moreover, why should anyone invest cognitive effort in deciding if a brand is a sponsor or ambusher? As observers have said about ambush marketing, "Don't kid yourself that consumers care" (Pitt et al. 2010).

In short, in memory research, the categories and definitions utilized by the industry may be meaningless to attendees and consumers. In fact, the categories that are useful to those investigating memory for sponsors may actually influence responses (Rosch & Mervis 1975). For example, cueing respondents about the level of a sponsor (anchor, mid-tier, low-tier) has been shown to influence the way in which they remember—if it doesn't seem appropriate to them or if they must think more carefully about the sponsor's level, their recall may be impacted (Wakefield et al. 2007).

Awareness of a sponsor–property relationship is a primary goal of sponsors in many contexts. At times it may be asking too much for consumers to remember this pairing with precision. It may be enough to positively influence in-store or online behavior. If a more nuanced understanding of the contribution of sponsorship to brand value is sought, then those measuring memory must not overemphasize the false recognition of foils as marketing failure. Instead, there is a need to invest in more sophisticated measures of memory in sponsorship and in the subsequent contexts of consumer behavior.

References

Bennett, R. (1999). Sports Sponsorship, Spectator Recall and False Consensus. *European Journal of Marketing*, *33*, 3/4, 291–313.

Cornwell, T. B. & Humphreys, M. S. (2013). Memory for Sponsorship Relationship: A Critical Juncture in Thinking. *Psychology & Marketing*, *30*, 5, 394–407.

Cornwell, T. B., Humphreys, M. S., Maguire, A. M., Weeks, C. S. & Tellegen, C. L. (2006). Sponsorship-linked Marketing: The Role of Articulation in Memory. *Journal of Consumer Research*, *33*, 3, 312–21.

Duke, C. R. & Carlson, L. (1994). Applying Implicit Memory Measures: Word Fragment Completion in Advertising Tests. *Current Issues and Research in Advertising*, *16*, 2, 29–39.

Herrmann, J.-L., Walliser, B., & Kacha, M. (2011). Consumer Consideration of Sponsor Brands they do not Remember: Taking a Wider Look at the Memorization Effects of Sponsorship. *International Journal of Advertising*, *30*, 2, 259–81.

Humphreys, M. S. & Bain, J. D. (1983). Recognition Memory: A Cue and Information Analysis. *Memory and Cognition*, *11*, 583–600.

Humphreys, M. S., Wiles, J. & Dennis, S. (1994). Toward a Theory of Human Memory Data Structures and Access Processes. *Behavioral and Brain Sciences*, *17*, 655–92.

Johar, G. V. & Pham, M. T. (1999). Relatedness, Prominence, and Constructive Sponsor Identification. *Journal of Marketing Research*, *36*, 3, 299–312.

Johar, G. V., Pham, M. T. & Wakefield, K. L. (2006). How Event Sponsors Are Really Identified: A (Baseball) Field Analysis. *Journal of Advertising Research*, *46*, 2, 183–98.

Kahneman, D. & Tversky, A. (1973). Availability: A Heuristic for Judging Frequency and Probability. *Cognitive Psychology*, *5*, 2, 207–32.

Keller, K. L. (1993). Conceptualizing, Measuring, and Managing Customer-based Brand Equity. *Journal of Marketing, 57*, 1, 1.

Lardinoit, T. & Derbaix, C. (2001). Sponsorship and Recall of Sponsors. *Psychology & Marketing, 18*, 2, 167–90.

Pitt, L., Parent, M., Berthon, P. & Steyn, P. G. (2010). Event Sponsorship and Ambush Marketing: Lessons from the Beijing Olympics. *Business Horizons, 53*, 281–90.

Quester, P. G. (1997). Awareness as a Measure of Sponsorship Effectiveness: The Adelaide Formula One Grand Prix and Evidence of Incidental Ambush Effects. *Journal of Marketing Communications, 3*, 1–20.

Reber, R., Winkielman, P. & Schwarz, N. (1998). Effects of Perceptual Fluency on Affective Judgements. *Psychological Science, 9*, 1, 45–8.

Rosch, E. & Mervis, C. B. (1975). Family Resemblances: Studies in the Internal Structure of Categories. *Cognitive Psychology, 7*, 4, 573–605.

Roy, D. P. & Cornwell, T. B. (2004). The Effects of Consumer Knowledge on Responses to Event Sponsorships. *Psychology & Marketing, 21*, 3, 185–207.

Schacter, D. L. (1987). Implicit Memory: History and Current Status. *Journal of Experimental Psychology: Learning, Memory, and Cognition, 13*, 3, 501–18.

Tripodi, J. A., Hirons, M., Bednall, D. & Sutherland, M. (2003). Cognitive Evaluation: Prompts Used to Measure Sponsorship Awareness. *International Journal of Market Research, 45*, 4, 435–55.

Wakefield, K. L., Becker-Olsen, K. & Cornwell, T. B. (2007). The Effects of Sponsorship Level, Prominence, Relatedness, and Cueing on Recall Accuracy. *Journal of Advertising, 36*, 4, 61–74.

Wentz, L. (2012). Consumers Don't Really Know Who Sponsors the Olympics. *Ad Age*, July 27. Retrieved October 26, 2013, from http://adage.com/article/global-news/consumers-sponsors-olympics/236367.

Zajonc, R. B. (1968). Attitudinal Effects of Mere Exposure. *Journal of Personality and Social Psychology*, Monograph Supplement, *9* (2, part 2), 1–27.

12

INTERNAL AUDIENCES FOR SPONSORSHIP

One of the areas where sponsorship has the largest unrecognized potential to contribute is in addressing internal audiences. Employees of a firm usually know about their company's sponsorships, but getting and keeping them onboard with the value of sponsoring is often neglected. Researchers in advertising have shown that when employees feel that their firm's advertisements are effective and aligned with their own personal values, their resultant pride encourages them to increase their customer focus and willingness to meet customer needs (Celsi & Gilly 2010). The potential to develop pride in sponsoring a sport or charity where employees could actually participate in the event might well have a greater impact than with advertising.

An early case study considered employee perceptions of the Bank of Ireland's sponsorship portfolio, which at the time included fine arts, music, and the Gaelic Football Championship (Grimes & Meenaghan 1998). The survey findings showed that while the sponsorships helped to develop pride in the organization and a feeling of being even more Irish, employees did not feel the sponsorships put any focus on staff. Importantly, they did not feel that the sponsorships made the bank a more desirable employer. This, as the authors note, might be due to individuals' particular expectations and experiences or because numerous factors influence a company's appeal, and what a company sponsors, may play only a minor role in employee perceptions.

Imagine a conversation at a bank with an employee on their sponsorship of the local symphony. If this individual feels that they are not included (or perhaps actively excluded) from the sponsored event he or she would not be likely to have something positive to say about it. On the other hand, if she had been given a free ticket to the symphony, or volunteered for it, she would likely feel more positive. If the internal audience member sees the fit of the sponsorship to corporate objectives, that too will foster a feeling of shared values and a sense of engagement. Thus, while sponsorships are recognized as having the potential to build a sense of corporate identity within the organization (Hickman et al. 2005), there must be internal marketing communications about the sponsorship to nurture identity building.

Employee engagement

Based on the premise that employee engagement drives shareholder return through lower staff turnover, increased productivity and profitability, as well as higher customer loyalty, Rogan (2008) identifies two important value streams stemming from sponsorship. First, there is a marketing stream, related to marketing activities and marketing outcomes that flows from sponsorship to employee engagement to customer service [quality], to consumer brand perception and preference, and on to sales and reduced customer churn. This path, depicted in Figure 12.1, views employee engagement as a boost to the consumer's experience. In terms of human resources, a flow from sponsorship that also includes employee engagement flows to employee attitudes and beliefs, employee behavior, and on to individual productivity, retention, and leadership (see Figure 12.2). This path views employee engagement as central to job satisfaction. Both of these paths arguably influence business performance.

Based on 22 in-depth interviews with senior marketing and sponsorship managers from six countries, researchers Farrelly and Greyser (2012) examined sponsorship-linked internal marketing and found many corporate identity and performance programs built around sport sponsorships. Most of these programs considered sport analogous to business, in ways such as reaching for one's personal best or building a team. They summarize the various programs as having one or more of the following orientations: identity and performance enhancing, strategy and planning-oriented, organization engagement development, leadership development, and rewards and goal setting.

How might large-scale employee engagement be fostered? Consider Aon and their "shirt" sponsorship of Manchester United football (soccer) club. Aon is a leading global provider of risk management, insurance and re-insurance brokerage, and human resources consulting solutions. This Fortune 500 company grew over the past 25 years through nearly 450 acquisitions. In keeping with their name, which means "oneness" in Gaelic, the company was in search of a common focus to connect its various acquired entities. In 2009 they announced, and in 2010 launched, a partnership with Manchester

FIGURE 12.1 Marketing pathway

Source: Adapted from Rogan (2008).

FIGURE 12.2 HR pathway

Source: Adapted from Rogan (2008).

United, one of the most valuable sport franchises in the world. Although the company was interested in brand awareness and increased business opportunities, they were particularly attracted to the potential of using Manchester United to unite more than 65,000 colleagues across 120 countries. To this end, they began by giving each employee his or her own Aon-branded Manchester United jersey.

A jersey, even one from a famous soccer team, is, however, not enough to develop engagement. To foster connectivity, Aon launched their "Pass It On" program for employees in 2011. Here, teams from Asia Pacific, Europe/Middle East/Africa, and the Americas competed for points as they passed along Manchester United soccer balls from city to city. Along the way community service activities with charity partners, client interactions, and colleague engagement grew. What have been the results stemming from the sponsorship? Here are some of the findings (Eckert 2012, 2013):

1. Pride among Aon-UK colleagues rose 24% from 2008 to 2010 at the beginning of the Aon/Manchester United partnership.
2. Seven in ten Aon employees think that the Manchester United partnership helps unite the firm.
3. Aon global service day (based on an Aon United platform) resulted in over 27,000 service hours via 280 activities with more than 280 charity partners. More than 8,000 colleagues participated in 46 countries.
4. The global engagement program of "Pass It On" had more than 45,000 employee participants in 88% of all Aon offices by hosting more than 525 local events.

After the success of the shirt sponsorship, Aon transitioned to an eight-year partnership to brand the club's training kit and rename the training grounds in Carrington, UK, as the Aon Training Complex. The relationship currently continues until 2021 and is, according to the BBC, estimated to be worth £15 million or about $25 million per season (Burnett 2013).

Employee identification as furthered by sponsorship

Social identity theory argues that as an individual becomes more deeply attached to an organization, the person becomes vested in the successes and failures of that organization (Ashforth & Mael 1989). Identification comes from a sense of shared values or value congruence (Hall & Schneider 1972) as well as links or mental connections between the organization and oneself (Dutton et al. 1994). Clearly, these are things that sponsorship could enhance. With this thinking in mind, it has been argued that employee identification with a firm can be furthered if there is an individual sense of meaning stemming from the sponsorships, the sponsorship program is viewed as effective, and if there is management support both in terms of commitment to the sponsorship and support for involvement in it (Coote & Cornwell 2004). In turn, identification with the firm should result in positive role behaviors important to the firm, such as supporting customer satisfaction, or spreading positive word-of-mouth about the firm and its sponsorship engagement.

Researchers Hickman et al. (2005) learned about the role of sponsorship in employee identification through the study of a NASCAR partnership held by a major trucking company. They set out to test whether employees with greater affinity for the firm's sponsored teams felt more identification with that company, and whether this affinity and identification led to organizational commitment and to a willingness to satisfy customers. Their study of more than 500 employees demonstrated that affinity for the firm's NASCAR sponsorship was indeed related to feelings of identification with the firm, commitment to the firm, and customer satisfaction.

One of the ways that sponsorship may build identification in the firm is through the development of perceptions of prestige (Khan & Stanton 2010). This notion, originating in management literature (Mael & Ashforth 1992), has been demonstrated in a consumer context (Cornwell & Coote 2005). Prestige has been the central focus in management but the word may be too narrow for all the perceptions of a firm that might support identification. A company that has cool products (e.g., Apple), or dynamic leadership (e.g., Amazon), or positive associations (e.g., Disney) may be just as capable along different lines to develop employee identification. Sponsorship could help to foster a wide range of identification-building relationships.

Employer branding

What, then, about future employees? They may be attracted to a potential employer, in part, by the sponsorships the company holds. Employer brand has been defined as "the package of functional, economic and psychological benefits provided by employment and identified with the employing company" (Ambler & Barrow 1996, p. 187). It includes all things associated with the firm in the mind of the potential employee, including what they sponsor. Although sponsorship may play only a small role in attracting new employees for most firms, the potential has been largely unexplored. If, however, a firm can fashion communications about its sponsorships that resonate with consumers, current employees, and potential future employees, then clearly there are efficiencies to be had.

As an example of an integrated communications platform, consider Canadian Tire's sponsorship of the Canadian Olympic Committee. The eight-year partnership, which launched in 2013, aims to build Canadian pride in the company for both external and internal audiences. Further, the partnership is envisioned as supporting jobs for athletes. Because athletic training requires flexible hours and sometimes flexibility in location, Canadian Tire sees its national network as able to accommodate these future employees.

Partner internal audiences

While discussions to this point have focused on the sponsoring organization's internal audience, it is important to remember that the partnering property being sponsored has an internal audience as well. How do the staff, team, or league feel about their sponsor? Are they proud to have this relationship or do they perceive that it is all about the money? Slipped comments and unfortunate tweets can undermine the belief of both consumers and the sponsors' employees regarding the authenticity of the relationship.

With the advent of the Word of Mouth Marketing Association's guidelines that sponsored tweets are marked with "#spon" there is the ability on the consumer's part to judge authenticity. It is, however, a dynamically evolving area of sponsorship. For example, Octavia Spencer, an actress known for her role in the movie *The Help*, was sponsored by Sensa weight loss systems. In her agreement, she was to comply with guidelines and make two social media posts per month. In a complaint she has filed, she claims that the company requested that she remove the "#spon" identifier from her tweets (Manatt Phelps & Phillips LLP 2013).

Most athletes are carefully trained to praise and recognize the support offered by a sponsor. While this may not always come across as a genuine acknowledgment, we can definitively say that negative comments toward the sponsor on the part of any representative of the property will do damage to the partnership. Even small missteps or in one instance a (mis)sip can be the end of a relationship. Coca-Cola-sponsored Brazilian soccer player, Ronaldinho, lost his sponsorship contract valued at $750,000 per year after taking a sip of Pepsi during a 2012 news conference (Tasch 2012). Individuals affiliated with a property are also cautioned not to engage in competing sponsorship. It has been reported that "Indian cricket captain Mahendra Singh Dhoni was rapped by the ICC for promoting and endorsing the products of Sony Corp and Aircel, which are not official sponsors of the Cup" (*The Indian Express* 2011). The complex web of sponsorship layers makes decisions on best communications practice by the partner, and all representatives of the partner an evolving art of discretion.

Capturing internal values

Perhaps the hardest question to answer on internal audiences is how does one measure the value of employee engagement or employer branding via sponsorship? This challenge likely explains why one sees little research in this area. It is difficult to say exactly what amount of increased sales or product inquiries results from a proud, more engaged employee. Farrelly & Greyser (2012) suggest that employee attitudes and identification can be measured, as can business outcomes. The challenge is developing a convincing link between employee engagement engendered by sponsorship and future outcomes for the brand. Unless a firm was committed to a longitudinal, total system analysis, the best approach would be to set objectives for interim steps or specific programs. For example, Farrelly & Greyser note that one of the firms in their study had found more customer complaints were resolved by employees after participation in a sponsorship-related learning and coaching program as compared to a control group that had no such training.

Employer branding outcomes related to sponsorship may be more easily tracked than employee engagement outcomes, especially online. For example, Aon's shirt sponsorship of Manchester United resulted in match-day traffic increases to Aon.com as high as 55% depending on the match. Further, traffic to Aon.com had the Aon careers webpage as the first click 3.1% of the time (Eckert 2013). Reducing the cost of talent acquisition might be one way to track the value of sponsorship. If individuals connect from their sport of interest to the sponsor, does this positive association support their exploration of the sponsor as an employer? It seems that longitudinal tracking could start to account for the internal marketing value of sponsorship.

References

Ambler, T. & Barrow, S. (1996). The Employer Brand. *The Journal of Brand Management, 4*, 3, 185–206.

Ashforth, B. E. & Mael, F. (1989). Social Identity Theory and the Organization. *Academy of Management, 14*, 1, 20–39.

Burnett, R. (2013). Ground Control: Manchester United to Rename Carrington "AON Training Complex" in £150m Sponsorship Deal. *Mirror Online.* Retrieved December 29, 2013 from http://www.mirror.co.uk/sport/football/news/manchester-united-rename-carrington-aon-1817815.

Celsi, M. W. & Gilly, M. C. (2010). Employees as Internal Audience: How Advertising Affects Employees' Customer Focus. *Journal of the Academy of Marketing Science, 38*, 520–9.

Coote, L. V. & Cornwell, T. B. (2004). Employee Identification with Sponsorship Programs: A Conceptual Framework of Antecedents and Outcomes. *American Marketing Association Winter Educators' Conference Proceedings, 15*, 305–6.

Cornwell, T. B. & Coote, L. V. (2005). Corporate Sponsorship of a Cause: The Role of Identification in Purchase Intent. *Journal of Business Research*, *58*, 3, 268–76.

Dutton, J. E., Dukerich, J. M. & Harquail, C. V. (1994). Organizational Images and Member Identification. *Administrative Science Quarterly*, *39*, 239–263.

Eckert, B. Personal communication, March 14, 2012.

Eckert, B. Personal communication, December, 2013.

Farrelly, F. & Greyser, S. (2012). Sponsorship Linked Internal Marketing (SLIM): A Strategic Platform for Employee Engagement and Business Performance. *Journal of Sport Management*, *26*, 506–20.

Grimes, E. & Meenaghan, T. (1998). Focusing Commercial Sponsorship on the Internal Audience. *International Journal of Advertising*, *17*, 51–74.

Hall, D. T. & Schneider, B. (1972). Correlations of Organizational Identification as a Function of Career Pattern and Organizational Type. *Administrative Science Quarterly*, *17*, 34, 340–50.

Hickman, T. M., Lawrence, K. E. & Ward, J. C. (2005). A Social Perspective on the Effects of Corporate Sport Sponsorship on Employees. *Sport Marketing Quarterly*, *14*, 3, 148–157.

Khan, A. M. & Stanton, J. (2010). A Model of Sponsorship Effects on the Sponsor's Employees. *Journal of Promotion Management*, *16*, 188–200.

Mael, F. & Ashforth, B. E. (1992). Alumni and Their Alma Mater: A Partial Test of the Reformulated Model of Organizational Identification. *Journal of Organizational Behavior*, *13*, 103–23.

Manatt Phelps & Phillips LLP (2013). Actress Claims Sponsorship Deal Sour over "#spon." *Lexology*, September 12. Retrieved November 27, 2013 from http://www.lexology.com/library/detail.aspx?g=236fb04f-686b-42c2-86a7-8afe95ffc906.

Rogan, M. (2008). Building the Business Case for Internal Sponsorship Activation. *Journal of Sponsorship*, *1*, 3, 267–73.

Tasch, J. (2012). Brazilian Soccer Legend Ronaldinho Loses Lucrative Coca-Cola Sponsorship Deal . . . for Sipping a Pepsi. *Daily News*. Retrieved November 27, 2013 from http://www.nydailynews.com/sports/more-sports/brazilian-soccer-legend-ronaldinho-loses-lucrative-coca-cola-sponsorship-deal-sipping-pepsi-article-1.1112211.

The Indian Express (2011). India Ambush Marketing Beating ICC. Retrieved November 27, 2013 from http://www.indianexpress.com/news/india-ambush-marketing-beating-icc/751882/.

13

PUBLIC POLICY AND SOCIAL RESPONSIBILITY IN SPONSORSHIP

Medical journal *The Lancet* opened its five-paper series on physical inactivity just a week before the start of the 2012 Olympic Games with the following editorial:

> The Games should encourage physical activity, promote healthy living, and inspire the next generation to exercise. However, marring this healthy vision has been the choice of junk food and drink giants— McDonald's, Coca-Cola, and Cadbury's—as major sponsors of the event.
>
> *The Lancet (2012, p. 188)*

It is easy to observe parallels between the tobacco industry and what one might call the "junk food" industry in relation to sponsorship. As threats of litigation and then enacted laws around the world ousted tobacco from broadcast advertising in the 1970s, that industry began to invest in sponsorship. A similar set of circumstances surrounds fast food, as countries propose bans on the advertising and marketing of calorie dense but nutritionally poor foods and drinks. Now, as the tobacco industry is being pushed from sponsorship by both policy and social outcry, the junk food industry appears to be taking its place.

In both situations public health is the pivotal issue, but the two categories are in fact distinct. Tobacco use is medically unhealthy in all circumstances, whereas with "junk food" the situation is less clearly defined. What classifies as junk food? Even if one can say that a particular product has no nutritional value, is it harmful with limited intake? Is the pairing of unhealthy foods with the healthy behavior of athletes misleading? Researchers are working on all these issues but from a marketing communications perspective, it may not be necessary to wait for the answers. If societal objections to the sponsorship of a sport by the "junk food" industry create enough negative publicity, at some point this negates the goodwill afforded by the sponsorship. Impressions of corporate social responsibility are lost when sponsorships are viewed as devious persuasion attempts that go against the public interest.

The interplay of public policy and corporate social responsibility

There are at least two reasons to consider public policy and corporate social responsibility in tandem when examining sponsorship. First, the development of public policy, or governmental actions that respond to public problems, has a long formative stage in countries where citizens and advocacy groups are able to have a voice in policy decisions. In this public preamble to law, especially in the area of marketing communications, sponsorship is an uncertain space where marketers can be active outside the more readily legislated areas such as broadcast communications. Another reason to consider public policy, corporate social responsibility, and sponsorship in the same breath is that governmental decisions about support for social causes influence the need for corporate support via sponsorship.

Public policy

Public policy is explained as government action designed to address issues of public concern. It may be at the local, state, federal, or international level. These public policy actions may be codified as law, or they may take the form of regulatory systems, or even funding priorities. In the negotiation of public policy, groups on many sides of an issue are involved in discussion. Before legislation is drafted and accepted into law, evidence in support of the various positions is typically sought. Business concerns are frequently involved in these dialogues, but beyond the conversations and the outcomes of those conversations, companies are becoming involved in actions oriented toward society. In some cases these actions may take the form of voluntary codes of conduct. In other instances, companies are proactively seeking opportunities to be part of the solution to social challenges—at times via sponsorship.

Corporate social responsibility (CSR)

Jane Nelson, policy analyst with the John F. Kennedy School of Government at Harvard University, describes corporate social responsibility as the way a company manages its overall impacts on and contributions to society through its core business operations, strategic philanthropy, and community investment and public policy dialogues, advocacy, and institution building (2008). The United States perspective on corporate social responsibility is elective, with some companies having strong, visible CSR programs and other companies choosing not to engage. In contrast, many other countries see CSR as an important corporate responsibility. In 2011, the European Commission on corporate social responsibility defined it as "the responsibility of enterprises for their impacts on society." Further, the European Commission states that to fully meet their social responsibility, enterprises "should have in place a process to integrate social, environmental, ethical human rights, and consumer concerns into their business operations and core strategy in close collaboration with their stakeholders" (European Commission 2011).

Corporate social responsibility approaches can be classified into four groups: political, integrative, ethical, and instrumental (Garriga & Melé 2004).

1. *Political* approaches to CSR use business power in responsible ways and are viewed as social duties and rights.
2. *Integrative* approaches to CSR combine social interests and business interests and recognize an integrating codependence between business and society.
3. The *ethical* approaches to CSR view businesses as holding an ethical obligation to society.
4. Lastly, the *instrumental* approaches to CSR view business as an instrument solely for wealth creation and CSR as a means to an end.

Corporate sponsorship often becomes part of the policy and law discussion in the form of corporate social responsibility. Expression of CSR under each of the four categories can be seen in sponsorship. Governance gaps and institutional failures create spaces, allowing companies to influence public policy for certain issues and industries. When government policies or financial support result in a gap between what society wants and what is currently being supplied, private enterprise may fill the void. The question left for marketers is how best to proceed.

The challenges of filling gaps

In 2006, the city of New Orleans, Louisiana, amended its city ordinance to permit corporate sponsorship of their Mardi Gras parades. Following the 2005 devastation from Hurricane Katrina, city and business leaders recognized that the financial challenge of hosting the event was too much for local constituents to bear. Researchers interested in the response of locals to a national corporate sponsorship interviewed 2,006 parade watchers after a national sponsor, Glad Products, was in place (Weinberger & Wallendorf 2012). They described reactions to the idea of corporate sponsorship as nuanced and complex. On one hand, local people recognized the financial need of the context but still viewed non-local corporations with trepidation. They summarized the feelings regarding corporate sponsorship of local community events as reflecting contemporary ambivalence but recognized that national or even international companies with a strong local presence may be viewed and accepted as local.

Sponsorship of social goods or programs can be viewed with suspicion. The Annual Report on Schoolhouse Commercializing Trends (Molnar et al. 2013) documents that US state governments faced with financial shortfalls are increasingly turning to sponsored programs, supplementary educational materials, and incentive programs. In their third year, the report documents and analyzes all manner of sponsorship and advertising within schools.

For example, the report accepts that Nestlé's Healthy Steps for Healthy Lives program meets core academic requirements but does so in a manner favorable to the company. Without mentioning the brand, Nestlé's "My Hydration Communication" lesson asks students to classify foods into food groups. Students learn about different food groups along with their need for water. Concepts such as "empty calories" and "moderation" are discussed. "Things get more interesting when the teacher is instructed to have the students brainstorm which other beverages they drink, and then determine which of those beverages 'count' toward the five servings of water they should have every day." The answer provided is: "They all count. Drinking water, water in beverages, and even water contained in food all contribute to total water intake. Some choices are better than others because of empty calories" (Molnar et al. 2013, p. 12). The overall recommendation stemming from the report is that "Policymakers should prohibit advertising in schools unless the school provides compelling evidence that their intended advertising program causes no harm to children" (p. 26).

Controversial products

Companies in industries such as tobacco, alcohol, firearms, gaming, and fast food have all received criticism for their sponsorship programs, particularly where the program involves sports or music. A central concern across these categories is the ability of those sponsored activities to reach youth audiences. Another significant concern is that adult products reach underage consumers readily via sponsorship. There are more specific concerns for combined pairs such as alcohol and auto racing, or martial arts with guns and ammunition.

Of all controversial products, research and discussions of restrictions on tobacco sponsorship is the most extensive. Concomitantly the effort by tobacco companies to find loopholes in restrictions and bans is the most elaborate.

Tobacco

Although a significant number of countries have enacted laws to limit tobacco advertising and sponsorship, many developing countries either do not have laws in place or do not enforce the laws they do have. Tobacco companies continue to circumnavigate legislation aimed at reducing tobacco promotion. When brands are well known for their name and imagery, as is the case with Marlboro and the Marlboro Man, brands go as far as setting up "shell" companies in unrelated industries to continue to legally advertise for clothes or shoes using established brand icons to avoid bans (Cornwell 1997). With the look and feel of the brand, and only the fine print to communicate the official product, the attribution to and reminder of tobacco products is easy.

The announcement of Marlboro's continued sponsorship of Formula One racing into 2015 seems at odds with the more extensive bans of brand information at sponsored events unless one looks more carefully at the overall marketing plan. For instance, international travelers are finding ". . . extra-ordinarily elaborate displays for products they did not know existed, being promoted under the brand names Ferrari and Scuderia Ferrari. In particular, a range of men's fragrances has caught the eye of some, who could not help noticing how the design of expensive looking boxes containing the perfume bears a striking resemblance to, well, the old Marlboro red and white chevron" (Simpson 2011, p. 323). The approach is to have surrogate reminders of past brand experience as well as to develop new links between the Ferrari F1 team through displays of Marlboro cigarettes where permitted.

Gambling and alcohol

Because gaming and gambling have had strong control against underage participation at the consumer level, these areas have not been as concerning in sponsorship as tobacco and alcohol. Still, the expansion of online betting has opened new worries of underage access and influence (Waugh 2006). Many feel that early exposure to gaming leads to future problems and this is one reason that there has been voluntary removal of betting logos from replica football shirts and kits for children (Drury 2007). On the other hand, some commentators feel that the fear of adult product sponsorships being seen by children is overestimated in terms of influencing future behaviors.

Commenting in 2009, Helen Day, Editor of the *Journal of Sponsorship* stated with regard to sponsorship exposure to children:

> Football has many alcohol and gambling sponsors, and children are sure to be aware of both their name and what they sell. There is no direct evidence that shows that such sponsorships encourage young people to drink more or start gambling, but these companies in particular need to be very careful and responsible about the impact of their sponsorships.
>
> *Day (2009, p. 298)*

Indeed, the author is correct that many studies are correlational and cross-sectional, which means that exposure or learning is documented but long-term behavioral change is not. For example, a study of 294 students aged 14 and 15 conducted in a Welsh city found that the number of alcohol sponsors recognized was positively correlated with likelihoods of both drinking and getting drunk (Davies 2009). The researchers critically examined the sporting culture where alcohol is ever present and concluded that alcohol sponsorships act as a "reinforcer" of attitudes that are already held rather than a direct instigator of behavior. What is needed, however, is longitudinal research that learns if young people receiving this support and endorsement of alcohol have different behavior patterns over time. Research that explains causal relationships would more clearly support policy decisions.

Researchers from Australia have brought into question the possible negative impact of gambling sponsorship in triggering problem gamblers. Utilizing a sample of 212 university students, their online survey showed that 63% of respondents became aware of one of 11 sports gambling companies via sponsorship. Of concern is that those scoring high on the Problem Gambling Severity Index were also more likely to intend to gamble and this was positively related to frequent viewing of sport containing gambling promotions and to receptivity to gambling sponsors' messages (Hing et al. 2013).

In a similar vein, another Australian study showed that sportspeople receiving alcohol sponsorships tended to have higher scores on measures of harmful drinking behavior (O'Brien et al. 2011). In contrast, sportspeople receiving non-alcohol sponsorships did not have the same measures of problem drinking. Further, the researchers controlled for early drinking behavior (namely reporting having been drunk before the age of 16). Thus, while there was a relationship, it was not that those already with a pattern of harmful drinking behaviors self-selected alcohol sponsorship.

Food and non-alcoholic drink

Research on the role of food and non-alcoholic drink sponsorships on health does not have background evidence that is as established as that on tobacco. There is research to say that opinions about fast food and liquor sponsorships are negative compared to sponsorship by sporting goods companies and water or sport drinks (Danyichuk & MacIntosh 2009). As with all marketing promotion, it is difficult to decouple the role of sponsorship from other forms of promotion.

From an industry report of NASCAR sponsorship there is evidence that sponsorship activations support an increase in average weekly consumption of soft drinks (DeGaris & West 2012). "On average, respondents who agree that the soft drink brand's sponsorship is effective consume about twice as much of the soft drink brand compared with respondents who do not agree that the sponsorship component is effective" (DeGaris & West 2012, p. 407). While we do not learn the history of these individuals and this data is not associated with health data, one can say that even if these individuals were already consumers of the product on a regular basis, the results suggest the sponsorship and sales promotion may have increased their intake.

Vulnerability

Children, the elderly, minority groups, and the poor are viewed as vulnerable groups across many contexts. Vulnerability implies that one is susceptible to injury or likely to succumb to persuasion and in need of protection. In sponsorship, children are of most concern. The World Health Organization has issued a Framework Convention on Tobacco Control (Article 13) that begins with the simple principle that it is well documented that tobacco marketing communications increase tobacco use and that comprehensive bans on tobacco communications decrease use. Yet internationally, tobacco companies target "starter markets" in the pivotal years of smoking onset (Dewhirst 2003). Smoking uptake in China begins on average at age ten and it has been suggested that this is in part due to the fact that more than 100 primary schools in China are now sponsored by tobacco companies (Moore 2011). The schools often are named after the cigarette brands and many have slogans such as "Talent comes from hard work—Tobacco helps you become talented"; the children wear branded uniforms and can buy single cigarettes from vendors near the school gates (Moore 2011).

Marketing directly to children (or even on them via their uniforms) seems more acceptable to parents if the product is, for example, sporting goods or healthy foods but unacceptable if alcohol (Kelly et al. 2012). Further, in a 2010 survey of 200 parents of children (aged 5–14) participating in a number of sports in Australia, they responded that snack food, fast food and confectionary companies were inappropriate as sponsors of sport (Kelly et al. 2012). Seven in ten of these parents (70%) supported restrictions on children's sport sponsorships, especially logos on children's uniforms. Interestingly, these researchers found that more parents thought children were influenced by the sponsorship of elite sport (86%) than of sponsorship of their own sport club (48%) (Kelly et al. 2012, p. 291).

Researchers from Austria found that children (aged 6–12) recognized 84% of the sponsors across the categories of snack food, bakery, bank, and supermarket (Grohs et al. 2012). These researchers concluded "sponsorship appears to be a highly effective communication tool for targeting children" but also noted that young children (under ten) found it difficult to understand sponsorship and therefore may need to be protected through learning about persuasive intent (Grohs et al. 2012, p. 915).

Companies seeking opportunities for socially responsible sponsoring will also encounter groups that may be considered vulnerable only in particular contexts. For example, people experiencing a natural disaster such as a tornado or earthquake are often labeled as vulnerable (Baker 2009). While the needs of vulnerable people present the socially responsible company with an opportunity to do good things, they need to proceed cautiously. Many but not all situations will include consumer behaviors that are related to the product categories where the company has offerings. This makes for a delicate situation where individuals may feel threatened or feel that the marketplace is preying on them (Baker et al. 2005). One alternative is for companies to sponsor fundraising events that are not directly tied to products. For example, following the 2010 Haiti earthquake where hundreds of thousands of people died and were injured, computer technology company Oracle became the presenting sponsor of the "Hit for Haiti" tennis exhibition at the BNP Paribas Open. This fundraising event raised $1 million for the American Red Cross Haiti Relief and Development fund.

Commercialization

Concern over the commercialization of sports may have seen its high water mark in the 1990s as sponsorship growth and, in particular, the growth of high visibility naming rights deals, made the news weekly. Most high profile of these naming rights deals was the 1995 change of Candlestick Park, home of the San Francisco NFL team, to 3Com Park. This was followed by a naming rights deal by Monster Cable, which resulted in the name of Monster Park. Following this agreement, and as result of a referendum that had been passed to restore the original name when the contract expired, the name returned to Candlestick Park in 2008. Community feelings of commercialization and resentment regarding the name changes may have carried over to the brands.

Concerns for commercialization of sport continue but sponsorship has become accepted as a business platform in sport. Currently, only egregious steps over invisible boundaries make the news. This does not mean that consumers' attitudes toward commercialism are not still influential. In fact, subtle or seemingly innocuous aspects of combining brand objectives with those of a sponsored entity can negatively influence brand perceptions.

Declining public support for the arts has left a financial gap that companies have partially filled via sponsorship. For example, major automakers such as Audi, BMW Group, DaimlerChrysler, and Volkswagen are regularly engaged in arts sponsorship (Schwaiger et al. 2010). Unlike sports, where sponsorship-linked marketing is generally accepted, there remains an uneasy tension in arts sponsorships. One can imagine the historic relationships established through public funds or philanthropy as being very different from the last few decades where quiet giving has been replaced by market-driven relationships.

As a case in point, the Henley Festival in the UK is a glamorous event that follows the Henley Regatta each summer. According to Finkel (2010), the Henley Festival showcases classical arts and is sponsored by a range of companies including many luxury good firms such as Lexus, Courvoisier, Whittard of Chelsea, and Sotheby's. Finkel argues, "reliance on business sponsorship has raised its exclusive status to include the corporate upper classes while 'pricing out' many in the community of classical arts enthusiasts" (p. 240). On the other hand, Finkel points out that in targeting the affluent, this type of sponsorship is very successful precisely because of this focus.

What a sponsor says and how they say it is important—commercialization of many events and activities is a given in terms of funding mechanisms, but the level of perceived commercialization is more related to marketing than it is to finance. Research examining the effectiveness of online activation found that the reason given for a sponsorship, and the articulated link between the sponsor and sponsee influences brand attitudes (Weeks et al. 2008). When the link between a brand (in this case adidas was the fictitious sponsor), and an event (sport or music), is cast as commercial (as the overlap between the audience for an event and that of the brand), rather than event-oriented (an opportunity to showcase sport or music talent), the attitudes toward the company were less favorable. The tone of the conversation around the sponsorship can build a link between the consumer and the brand or it can raise suspicion about the authenticity of the relationship. Consumers know that the brand is benefiting from the sponsorship, but if there is not a sense of balance or integration of event goals and brand goals, attitudes may be negative.

Consumer defense mechanisms

As we have seen, marketing communications gains can be erased when consumer defenses are aroused and brands are viewed as being commercial or inauthentic in their sponsor role. It is well established that there is a switch in one's mindset when a persuasion attempt is identified (Friestad & Wright 1994). A red flag of sorts goes up in a person's mind when he or she feels that there is an attempt to push them in a direction. While not fully researched yet, the public commentary surrounding the combining of, for example, a healthy sport with unhealthy food and drink, might be the tip of the communications iceberg if the vast majority of people are skeptical about the relationship.

Goodwill and positive attitude resulting from sponsorships rests on correspondence bias or the tendency of people to think that people or firms are as they act (Gilbert & Malone 1995). If a company supports a healthy activity, they must be health-oriented, if a company engages in a charitable cause, they must be charitable. The disruption of this natural way of thinking stems from aroused suspicion (e.g., Fein & Hilton 1994). Thus, if a brand is engaged in a sponsorship where many people become suspicious, the result could be that there is a loss of brand meaning on both the part of the sponsor and the property (Pappu & Cornwell 2014). How does this happen?

Any brand or corporation that has an "aligned difference" or a point where there is a similarity but that the two entities may be at opposite ends of a continuum (Markman & Gentner 1996) presents the potential for skepticism in sponsorship. For example, an oil company sponsoring environmental protection or a fast food restaurant sponsoring breast cancer research may align on "environment" or "health" but be at opposite positions in terms of people's perceptions.

Across three studies using real brands but hypothetical sponsor–sponsee pairings, the role of skepticism and the breakdown of natural correspondence bias have been shown to be influential when a cause is sponsored (Pappu & Cornwell 2014). In the case of quick service restaurants, these businesses have been shown to have a natural alignment with "health" as does a charity such as the Red Cross. If the restaurant offers calorie dense, nutrient poor foods, this is an aligned difference, with similarity between the two in terms of a connection to health, but a poor fit. However, if the restaurant offers foods viewed as healthy, such as the case with the Subway brand, their sponsorship of a group like the Red Cross is perceived as both similar and fitting.

If the relationship is viewed as having a basis of similarity and if the fit between the two is compelling, the sponsor and the sponsored will likely be viewed positively and with a sense of clear brand meaning. If people view the sponsorship as exploitative (there is similarity that may be related to a hidden agenda—making an unhealthy food appear healthy), then the fit is poor and both the sponsoring brand and the sponsored property will suffer. It is, however, the case that those most skeptical consumers may not be the ones in the target audience for quick service foods. This is perhaps how these poor fitting sponsorship relationships continue to be viewed as strategically valuable.

Unless specifically examined and addressed, this negative result of sponsoring against public opinion is difficult to gauge. When the outcry is public and the debate roiling, there is information for decision-making. For instance, the Kentucky Fried Chicken (KFC) sponsorship of the Susan G. Koman Race for the Cure to fight breast cancer met with considerable public backlash (Black 2010). The "Buckets for the Cure" campaign was widely criticized based on the relationship between unhealthy diets and the incidence of breast cancer. Research shows, however, that far subtler failures of fit influence brand and property sponsorship outcomes (Pappu & Cornwell 2014). Given the endless ways that a brand can communicate with an audience, it seems an unnecessary risk to combine a product and a property in a manner that creates negative publicity, or that raises suspicion in the mind of potential consumers, and quietly but negatively impacts brand equities.

References

Baker, S. M. (2009). Vulnerability and Resilience in Natural Disasters: A Marketing and Public Policy Perspective. *Journal of Public Policy & Marketing, 28*, 1, 114–23.

Baker, S. M., Gentry, J. W. & Rittenburg, T. L. (2005). Building Understanding of the Domain of Consumer Vulnerability. *Journal of Macromarketing, 25*, 2, 128–39.

Black, R. (2010). Eat Fried Chicken for the Cure? KFC's Fundraiser with Susan G. Komen Group Raises Some Eyebrows. *New York Daily News*, April 22. Retrieved December 29, 2013 from http://www.nydailynews.com/life-style/health/eat-fried-chicken-cure-kfc-fundraiser-susan-g-komen-group-raises-eyebrows-article-1.166080.

Cornwell, T. B. (1997). The Use of Sponsorship-linked Marketing by Tobacco Firms: International Public Policy Issues. *Journal of Consumer Affairs, 31*, 2, 238–54.

Danyichuk, K. E. & MacIntosh, E. (2009). Food and Non-Alcoholic Beverage Sponsorship of Sporting Events: The Link to the Obesity Issue. *Sport Marketing Quarterly, 18*, 2, 69–80.

Davies, F. (2009). An Investigation into the Effects of Sporting Involvement and Alcohol Sponsorship on Underage Drinking. *International Journal of Sports Marketing and Sponsorship, 11*, 1, 25–45.

Day, H. (2009). Protecting the Innocent from Sponsorship? *Journal of Sponsorship, 2*, 4, 296–9.

DeGaris, L. & West, C. (2012). The Effects of Sponsorship Activation on the Sales of a Major Soft Drink Brand. *Journal of Brand Strategy, 1*, 4, 403–12.

Dewhirst, T. (2003). Intertextuality, Tobacco Sponsorship of Sports, and Adolescent Male Smoking Culture: A Selected Review of Tobacco Industry Documents. *Journal of Sport and Social Issues, 27*, 4, 372–98.

Drury, I. (2007). Gambling Sponsors "Erased" from Children's Replica Football Shirts. *MailOnline*. Retrieved November 12, 2013 from http://www.dailymail.co.uk/news/article-473951/Gambling-sponsors-erased-childrens-replica-football-shirts.html.

European Commission (2011). Communication from the Commission to the European Parliament, the Council, The European Economic and Social Committee and the Committee of the Regions: A Renewed EU Strategy 2011–2014 for Corporate Social Responsibility, COM(2011) 681.

Fein, S. & Hilton, J. L. (1994). Judging Others in the Shadow of Suspicion. *Motivation and Emotion, 18*, 2, 167–98.

Finkel, R. (2010). Re-imaging Arts Festivals through a Corporate Lens: A Case Study of Business Sponsorship at the Henley Festival. *Managing Leisure, 15*, 237–50.

Friestad, M. & Wright, P. (1994). The Persuasion Knowledge Model: How People Cope with Persuasion Attempts. *Journal of Consumer Research, 21*, 1, 1–31.

Garriga, E. & Melé, D. (2004). Corporate Social Responsibility Theories: Mapping the Territory. *Journal of Business Ethics, 53*, 51–71.

Gilbert, D. T. & Malone, P. S. (1995). The Correspondence Bias. *Psychological Bulletin, 117*, 1, 21–38.

Grohs, R., Wagner, U. & Steiner, R. (2012). An Investigation of Children's Ability to Identify Sponsor and Understand Sponsorship Intentions. *Psychology & Marketing, 29*, 11, 907–17.

Hing, N., Vitartas, P. & Lamont, M. (2013). Gambling Sponsorship of Sport: An Exploratory Study of Links with Gambling Attitudes and Intentions. *International Gambling Studies, 13*, 3, 281–301.

Kelly, B. L., Baur, A., Bauman, A. E., King, L., Chapman, K. & Smith, B. J. (2012). Restricting Unhealthy Food Sponsorship: Attitudes of the Sporting Community. *Health Policy, 104*, 288–95.

Markman, A. B. & Gentner, D. (1996). Commonalities and Differences in Similarity Comparisons. *Memory and Cognition, 24*, 2, 235–49.

Molnar, A., Boninger, F., Harris, M. D., Libby, K. M. & Fogarty, J. (2013). Promoting Consumption at School: Health Threats Associated with Schoolhouse Commercialism. *The Fifteenth Annual Report on Schoolhouse Commercializing Trends: 2011–2012*. Boulder, CO: National Education Policy Center.

Moore, M. (2011). Chinese Primary Schools Sponsored by Tobacco Firms. *The Telegraph*, September 21. Retrieved October 4, 2013 from http://www.telegraph.co.uk/news/worldnews/asia/china/8779180/Chinese-primary-schools-sponsored-by-tobacco-firms.html.

Nelson, J. (2008). CSR and Public Policy: New Forms of Engagement between Business and Government. *Corporate Social Responsibility Initiative Working Paper No. 45*. Cambridge, MA: John F. Kennedy School of Government, Harvard University.

O'Brien, K. S., Miller, P. G., Kolt, G. S., Martens, M. P. & Webber, A. (2011). Alcohol Industry and Non-Alcohol Industry Sponsorship of Sportspeople. *Alcohol and Alcoholism, 46*, 2, 210–13.

Pappu, R. & Cornwell, T. B. (2014). Sponsorship as an Image Platform: Understanding the Roles of Relationship Fit and Sponsor-Sponsee Similarity. *Journal of the Academy of Marketing Science*, forthcoming.

The Lancet (2012). Chariots of Fries. *The Lancet*, July 21, *380*, 9838, 188.

Schwaiger, M., Sarstedt, M. & Taylor, C. R. (2010). Art for the Sake of the Corporation: Audi, BMW Group, DaimlerChrysler, Montblanc, Siemens, and Volkswagen Help Explore the Effect of Sponsorship on Corporate Reputations. *Journal of Advertising Research*, March, 77–90.

Simpson, D. (2011). World: New Marlboro F1 Sponsorship—But Why? *Tobacco Control*, *20*, 5, 323–6.

Waugh, N. (2006). Game Over for Gambling Sponsors. *Marketing Week*, December 21, 10.

Weeks, C. S., Cornwell, T. B. & Drennan, J. C. (2008). Leveraging Sponsorships on the Internet: Activation, Congruence, and Articulation. *Psychology & Marketing*, *25*, 7, 637–54.

Weinberger, M. F. & Wallendorf, M. (2012). Intracommunity Gifting at the Intersection of Contemporary Moral and Market Economies. *Journal of Consumer Research*, *39*, 74–92.

COMPANIES AND PROPERTIES INDEX

SUBJECT INDEX

Made in the USA
Lexington, KY
01 February 2019